11.

A new approach to the theory of international trade

Dr. C. J. RIJNVOS
Professor of Economics, Erasmus University Rotterdam

Martinus Nijhoff | The Hague 1976

Translated by A. M. H. Speller

ISBN 90.247.1851.1

Printed in the Netherlands.

CONTENTS

VI. International equilibrium at comparative cost differences

Translations into English of foreign titles are provided in the index

INTRODUCTION

Seen from a methodological point of view, the practice of economic science includes critical and theoretical thinking. The specific nature of these fields of study, their limitations and mutual adjustment have been covered by us elsewhere.[1] It became apparent that critical thinking aims at reaching a logical data description, simplifying social economic reality. Based on these data, it is the task of theory to discover logical laws in economic activity, if this is realized in a rational manner – and this is naturally a theoretical-analytical condition. Economic science according to this structure can be seen in the diagram below. A more extensive summary is provided in the synopsis of 'valuation of economic science', at the end of this study.

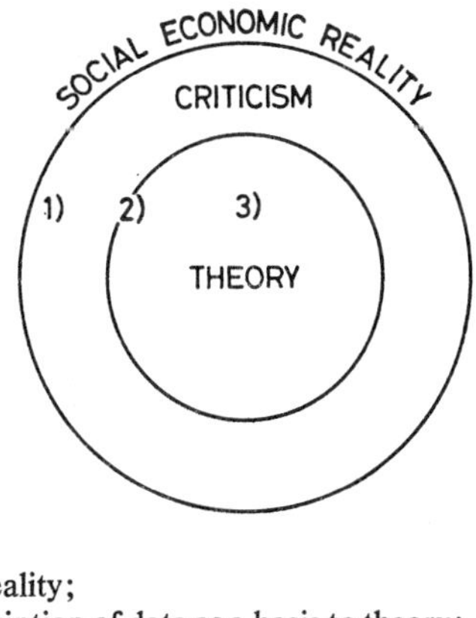

1. appraisal of economic reality;
2. a logical consistent description of data as a basis to theory;
3. formulation of tendencies in economic process.

A science pursued with this objective may fall short in two ways. In the first instance, it is possible that the critical thinking is too far divorced from reality. The data from which in this instance conclusions are made, are unrealistic; they are probably too idealistic. In this way a basis is laid for the

1. See our study *Waardering van het economisch denken*. More particular Chapter IV.

futile formulation of laws in a presupposed economic process, because the conclusions of science are very far from reality. In that case, the theory is nothing more than a 'set of assertions' without empirical confirmation; and which according to the present philosophy of science, cannot be rated very highly.[2] This manner of thinking results in science and practice being largely separated. The methodological stipulation that theory must reflect practise in order that economic science gets its meaning, is then ignored. Secondly, the strictly theoretical analysis may fall short; this occurs if it does not proceed entirely in accordance with the rules of logical thinking. In that situation something is wrong in the verbal-rationally or mathematically inclined manner of examination. It is obvious that this contains a methodological deficiency as it means a description of economic laws in a manner which is not rationally reliable. The starting point for this study is that present economic science does not meet the methodological requirements outlined here. As a rule, only general, obvious data – such as utility and profit maximization, plus production factors to a certain extent, and with a certain technical suitability – serve as data for the theory. By this the area indicated by 1) in the diagram is not entered. Economic science based on assessing initial points which are not open for discussion, is a strictly logical analysis, within which only the second – just mentioned form of criticism is possible. Indeed, in many cases economic thinking concerns not much more than a system of assertions, with pretended 'freedom of value'* rated highly. We departed here from that methodological limitation. The guideline for this study is the fact that the objective of economic science consists of an appreciative and rational probing into the social-economic reality. As for the method, the emphasis is on the relationship between criticism and theory of the economic scientific manner of examination. The reason for this is that the correct adjustment of critical and theoretical thinking to one another has the objective that the data must offer a possibility of an all-round sensible theoretical analysis within the framework of the problem. In principle this is simple and obvious. Just as writing a letter (considered as a problem) requires pen, ink and paper, so the theoretical description of consumer behaviour – by way of example – cannot be done without a clear insight into

2. J. J. Klant, *Spelregels voor economen.* Chapter I.

* *Translator's note:* The German concept 'Wertfreiheit' or the Dutch 'waardevrijheid' has no precise English equivalent. In the English text the expression 'freedom of value' has been used in the sense that the theory is not influenced by the social philosophy held by the scientist.

incomes, prices and preferences.[3] Equally, any form of economic thinking needs a minimum data-set, in which critical thinking, must be provided.

With this elementary methodological requirement constantly in the background – which is simply a correct description of the data as the basis for theoretical thinking – our study concerns the theory of international trade and in particular the theory of comparative costs. As is well known, the latter is a classic doctrine in the theory of international economic relations. This study covers the period from Ricardo onwards.

However, international trade includes more than the theory of comparative costs, even when freed from economic, political and monetary considerations. The comparative cost theory starts from the assumption that in countries involved in the analysis, the costs ratio vary, whereas the means of production are suitable for re-allocation, in the sense that they may serve for the production of all final products which are internationally traded. In chapter IV, the possibility of re-allocation has not been preassumed. This results in the description of a process of international trade, which differs considerably from what occurs when comparative cost differences exist. If the means of production cannot be re-allocated, trade across frontiers leads to substitution of the final products. This form of international trade is an essential part of the model to be constructed. It is important to treat it separately, as so far it has usually been mixed in a methodologically undesirable manner with theory of comparative costs. However, apart from this, our main attention is concentrated on the theory of comparative costs, which is methodologically carefully criticized. In this manner this book differs from a recent study of the theory of international trade, produced by Ketting. In his treatment no examination has been provided of the 'usefulness of a theory'.[4] Our work is indeed directed towards such an examination. Matters which were left unsaid by Ketting, will be emphasized by us.

When the specified conditions – which are differences in comparative costs and the ability to re-allocate the factors of production – have been met, one can proceed to specialization of production and international trade for the benefit of each participating country. A sensible, three-fold analysis of the comparative cost theory can now be set out as follows:

- with which exchange ratio between the participating countries can the optimum exchange advantage be achieved?
- to what extent will the production in each country be specialized?
- what quantities of final products will then be traded?

3. See Erich Scheider, *Einführung in die Wirtschaftstheorie*. Part II, Chapter I.
4. A. Ketting, *Inleiding tot de handelstheorie*. Pg. VII.

Inevitably these questions involve a certain subjective element which always characterizes the pursuit of science, resulting in a study never being strictly objective. Moreover, it is fitting to make as an introductory remark the fact that the calculation of the exchange advantage must finally be based on value considerations, which are decisive for economic thinking and action in the prevailing social system. The concept of value as a basis for economic scientific thinking is of philosophical origin. The philosophy reflects on the 'orientation of life'[5], which is why within the boundaries of philosophy and economics a reflection on economic values of life is possible. Naturally, more or less sharp contradictions are not excluded from this. A certain controversy also plays a part in this study, namely the one between the labour and the subjective theory of value.

In the marxist labour theory of value, the above orientation has an objective tendency, in the sense that economic values are considered in principle as being independent from subjective human considerations. Contrary to this in the marginal utility school the theory of value goes explicitly in the subjective direction. Some classical economists – more precisely Adam Smith and David Ricardo – accepted a specific form of the labour theory of value before the development of the marginal utility school. Additionally, Ricardo developed, practically for the first time, the comparative cost theory. Unavoidably, this two-fold procedure led to some confusion. Within the comparative cost theory the labour value theory was applied and that was a breeding ground for later tensions. In chapter II we shall methodologically examine this issue. This will lead to the conclusion that the labour value theory is not suitable as a basis for the comparative cost theory, in order to provide a reply to the three above questions.

In the meantime, the discussion between pure objectivists and pure subjectivists belong practically to the past in western economy science. Objectively pure versus subjectively pure is nothing more than a feigned contrast for the economy of the mixed economic system. A product has an economic value, because it supplies a want. Only based on this can one differentiate. The value may obtain the predicate 'objective' in the production sector and be indicated as 'subjective' in the consumptive sphere. As aspects of economic value, both the objective and the subjective recognize each other and only exist by virtue of that mutuality.

In the theory of international-economic relations, this plays an important part and greatly affects our study. This is already apparent from the rough outlines of the entire matter. The study of comparative costs is based on the

5. See M. G. Plattel, *Sociale Wijsbegeerte*. I - pg. 9.

theory of value described above, and by preparing the data to provide answers to problems of the optimum exchange ratio, the specialization of production and the bulk of international trade.

Gradually in the evaluation of the manner in which the comparative cost doctrine developed over a period of time, the data description acquires two specific characteristics. In the first place and in close connection with the above value concept, it includes a stable place for production and consumption, especially with regard to one another. The second characteristic concerns a correct introduction of micro and macro economic matters. In both points the approach shows shortcomings so far. Consequently, throughout the history of the theory of international-economic relations there exists a methodologically incomplete treatment of comparative costs. The following four phases can be distinguished:

- Only in a micro-economic way did Ricardo observe the production sector. He used the labour theory of value as a foundation. This rendered it impossible to indicate an optimum exchange ratio and the corresponding production specialization plus the bulk of international trade;
- A contrasting one-sidedness is shown by the methods of approach of Mill and Marshall. Admittedly, attention has been paid to the consumption sector and the subjective value aspect, but production remained more or less outside the field of vision. In fact, the considerations are outside the comparative cost theory;
- The analysis by Edgeworth can be seen as an attempt to synthesis. It did not succeed entirely, as it omitted to use re-allocatable production factors as a basis, whereas these are essential for the comparative cost differences. In fact, Mill, Marshall and Edgeworth have described international trade by substitution of final products;
- Especially with the concave transformation curve, Heckscher/Ohlin and Haberler provide a mix-form of final product substitution (without the ability to re-allocate resources) comparative cost differences (with re-allocatable resources). Also this approach omits the possibility of indicating theoretically within the comparative cost theory the optimum exchange ratio production specialization and international trade. Additionally, an examination based on the Heckscher/Ohlin principle remains entirely inside the methodological scope of the neo-classical economy, as a result of which it is not possible to connect the comparative cost theory in a correct manner with the growth theory and the theory of income distribution.

Despite the methodological incompleteness the stated treatments are of great importance; each contribution contains a building brick for the design of an all-round theory of the international trade. In our attempt to synthesis we do not do much more than put these bricks together.

1. ANALYSIS VIEWED FROM THE PRODUCTION SECTOR

The methodologically-incomplete rendering of the comparative cost theory had already commenced at the beginning of the last century. Though Torrens had already drawn attention to the possible advantages to be derived from the existence of differences in comparative costs it was Ricardo who dealt extensively with this subject in his main work. At that point our study commences.

1. Ricardo

The famous pages in 'Principles' according to which 'the same rule which regulates the relative value of commodities in one country does not regulate the relative value of the commodities between two or more countries'[1] as a rule form the beginning of the theory of international trade. Exchange within a closed national economy progresses according to Ricardo in accordance with the rules of the relative labour cost theory of value in such a way that the labour which must be applied for the production of a commodity determines the exchange value.

'If the quantity of labour realized in commodities regulates their exchangeable value, every increase of the quantity of labour must augment the value of that commodity on which it is exercised, as every diminution must lower it'.[1]

However, this is only the case given complete mobility of the production factors. Ricardo considers this to be possible within a specific country, but not between countries. This initial point plays an essential part in the Ricardian law of comparative costs; it is a fortunate circumstance that this is quite clearly formulated in the 'Principles' – at least in so far as it concerns the factor of capital: 'If the profits of capital employed in Yorkshire should ex-

1. David Ricardo, *The Principles of Political Economy and Taxation*. Pg. 81, 7, 81-82 resp.

ceed those of capital employed in London, capital would speedily move from London to Yorkshire, and an equality of profits would be effected; but if in consequence of the diminished rate of production in the lands of England from the increase of capital and population wages should rise and profits fall, it would not follow that capital and population would necessarily move from England to Holland, or Spain or Russia, where profits might be higher'.[2]

To illustrate the possible advantages which can be achieved by production specialization and international trade with comparative cost differences, Ricardo uses a well-known example, as shown in table 1.

Table 1. Ricardian version of comparative cost theory.

Required amount of labour		
for and in ⟶	England	Portugal
↓		
volume of wine	120	80
volume of cloth	100	90

To obtain advantages, England concentrates on the production of cloth and Portugal on the production of wine. Subsequently, and in accordance with the presentation of matters in 'Principles', an x-quantity of wine is exchanged for a y-quantity of cloth, which is advantageous to both countries. As soon as Ricardo starts discussing mutual advantages, the treatment of the comparative cost theory becomes somewhat double-edged and loses in clarity. On the one hand the author of 'Principles' relinquishes the relative labour cost doctrine, which is once more explicitly stated: 'The quantity of wine which she (i.e. Portugal) shall give in exchange for the cloth of England is not determined by the respective quantities of each, as it would be if both commodities were manufactured in England, or both in Portugal'. This is one side of the argument, the other side is the manner in which the advantage to be achieved is indicated. The 'Principles' are not entirely clear regarding this, but the criterion of labour saving is most obvious: 'To produce the wine in Portugal might require only the labour of 80 men for one year, and to produce the cloth in the same country might require the labour of 90 men for the same time. It would therefore be advantageous for her to export wine in exchange for cloth'. The example indicates clearly the advantage in the form of labour saving. England relinquishes a y-quantity of cloth, which has cost 100 labour units and receives in return x-quantity of wine, which, if

2. David Ricardo, *The Principles of Political Economy and Taxation.* Pg. 81, 7, 81-82 resp.

produced in England, would have required 120 units of labour. Consequently, the advantage for England is 20 labour units. Portugal relinquishes an x-quantity of wine, which required 80 labour units in production and receives in return a y-quantity of cloth values – which would have required 90 labour units to produce in Portugal – a saving of 10 labour units.

As a result of the indicated dualism – with on the one side relinquishing the labour cost theory of value and on the other side the accepting of labour saving as a criterion for the exchange advantage – two points demand further attention. In the first place it is essential to search for the solution of a certain amount of obscurity in international trade theory as several authors hold the opinion – despite his denial – that Ricardo bases the theory of comparative costs on the labour cost theory of value. Secondly there is the question as to whether it is possible to adequately solve, with the application of the principle of labour saving, the basic questions of the comparative cost doctrine – which relate to the correct external exchange ratio, the degree of production specialization and the volume of international trade. We will not investigate this further now since the two questions form the subject of the next chapter. In this section we limit our study to the significance of Ricardo's line of thought without considering as such the labour theory of value and the criterion of labour saving. However, it will be expedient to use the following symbols:

I, II, ...	=	different countries
$c_1, c_2, \ldots$	=	final products
α	=	labour coefficient

Here the labour coefficient has been defined as a fraction within the numerator, the labour necessary for the production of the final product stated in the denominator. If the coefficient relates to a specific country, it is preceded by suffix I, II, ...; in a sectoral indication it acquires in addition $c_1, c_2, \ldots$

The main issue in Ricardo's argument is the fact that cost ratio vary from country to country. Indeed, these are of fundamental importance to the theoretical description of the trade between countries. For a further study of Ricardo's argument, the internal exchange rate curves (I_R^{I} or I_R^{II} resp.) of figure 1 are instructive. These curves have the characteristic that at each point of them an equal amount of labour has been used for the production of c_1 and c_2. The non-coincidence of the I_R-curves of the countries concerned indicates the existence of comparative cost differences.

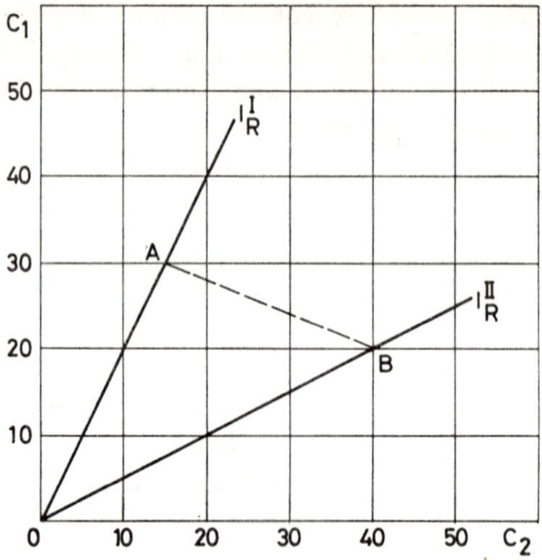

Fig. 1. Internal exchange ratios.

Irrespective of the absolute cost levels, the curves coincide when these differences are absent, and it is impossible to achieve labour saving as described above by production specialization and international trade. This can be explained with the aid of table 2.

Table 2. Comparative cost ratios.

labour coefficient \ countries	I	II
α_{c_1}	2	4
α_{c_2}	1	2

The sole exchange relation at which there is no labour loss for either of the two countries at the quoted labour coefficients, is $c : 2c_2$. It is now the same on whichever product the various countries concentrate; the result is always the same. Let us assume that country I selects c_1, whereas country II prefers c_2. Country I releases c_1, which cost 2 labour units and receives in return 2 c_2 of an equal value. The reverse image of this is that country II exchanges 2 c_2

for c_1, both of which have for the country concerned a value of four labour units. All this implies that at comparative cost ratios international trade with no labour saving can be achieved for all participating countries. This conclusion also applies to criteria other than labour saving ones dealt with later in this study; however, we shall not refer then to the case of comparative cost relations. The situation is such that in the event of equal cost relations the I_R-curves simply coincide; in that situation there is no opportunity for an external exchange relationship on which mutually advantageous trade could be based. Labour saving – or according to another criterion advantageous trade between countries is only possible when the production factors can be re-allocated with an external exchange ratio between I_R-curves.

Ricardo's theory implicitly includes the I_R-curves as limits for the external exchange relation; however, a further description of the latter is not provided in the 'Principles'. De Roos gives the impression that Ricardo did not search for this either in a scientific manner. He studied international trade mainly through the eyes of the trader and held the opinion 'that the precise point of exchange would be determined by the adroitness of purchasers and sellers'.[3] Consequently, Ricardo's theory is, in fact, limited to the indication of production conditions in order to proceed in the event of re-allocatable production factors with mutual advantage to production specialization and international trade. The Ricardian line of thought falters in the micro-economic aspect of the production sector, owing to the fact that the quantitative dimension of the production factors as macro-data plus the consumption sector, were not included in the examination, together with the fact that the criterion of labour saving still raises many questions. It can be concluded from this that the line of thought in the 'Principles' has not been developed to include the optimum exchange ratio. In addition Ricardo's study does not provide an answer to the question as to what extent each country will go in production specialization and what quantities of final product will then be internationally traded.

2. Harrod

At a later stage many authors tried to work out further the comparative cost theory with regard to three essential points. Whale's work is an example of this. This study concerns a further investigation of the path of the external

3. F. de Roos, *Theorie van de internationale economische betrekkingen.* Pg. 127.

exchange curve in the Ricardian way of thought.[4] It includes a rather sharp criticism of the manner of approach by Mill and Marshall which will be discussed later. Whale asserts – without very good reasons – that for the determination of the optimum external exchange ratio 'the earlier exponents of the theory (i.e. Mill and Marshall) could suggest no better answer than that it depends upon "the higgling of the market" – in other words on bluff'. Furthermore, Whale thinks he has found the key to a simple and correct solution: 'The problem would become more determinate in some cases if we abandoned the assumptions of constant costs'. Whale expands on this subject a little. However, we shall not investigate this as the search for the optimum exchange ratio based on non-constant costs has been worked out far more penetratingly by Harrod.[5]

First of all, in an attempt to indicate the optimum exchange ratio based on non-constant costs, attention is directed towards the effect of the law of the non-proportional returns. This involves a certain extension of Ricardo's line of thought, as here labour is earmarked as the sole production factor. After all, the effect of the law of non-proportional returns implies the application of at least two factors of production, one of which can be varied and the other remaining constant (or at least, varying relatively little). In Harrod's analysis this difference cannot be seen very clearly, as he takes into account only the development of the total costs per unit.

In developing this line of thought Harrod observes as a hypothetical example that in Britain the cost of a unit of wheat and a unit of coal relate as 1 : 1. Abroad this ratio is 1 : 5, consequently, there are comparative cost differences. It is obvious that under these circumstances Britain will specialize in the production of coal. During the realization of this specialization, the costs per unit of coal will increase and those of wheat fall, owing to the effect of the law of non-proportional returns. This is possible when labour which was used until then for the production of wheat, is released for the production of coal. As a result of this the production per employee in the agricultural sector will increase but will decrease in the mining sector. Harrod assumes implicitly here an effect of the part of the law of non-proportional returns – when the costs per unit increase as production is increased. Under the influence of that the original cost ratio in Britain will change after some time to, for example, 1 : 2. Abroad, as a result of a differently directed specialization, a reverse development takes place. There, with the extension of the wheat production and a reduction of the coal production a cost ratio of, for exam-

4. Barret Whale, *International Trade*. Pg. 107.
5. R. Harrod, *International Economics*. Pg. 20-23.

ple, 1 : 4 is achieved. The significance of the theory now becomes clear. Production specialization and international trade include a tendency to uniformity of cost ratios. Finally these will become equal. From that moment onwards production specialization and international trade are no longer a proposition; the limits of both have been reached.

For an assessment of Harrod's theory we shall first investigate the circumstances under which the indicated effect of the law of the non-proportional returns can take place. The first condition is, as we have seen already, a combination of at least two production factors, which are subsequently varied in an unequal manner. When will this form of allocation become of importance to production specialization and international trade? Theoretical accuracy requires here a precise description of the possibilities regarding the nature of the means of production. A three-fold differentiation is possible:

- the production factors are not re-allocatable. Consequently, they can only be applied to the production of c_1 or of c_2. In this situation it is impossible to proceed to production specialization and international trade based on differences in cost ratios. In so far as trade between countries takes place, it consists of substitution of final products. This subject is further dealt with in chapter IV. It will there become apparent that in this form of international trade the external exchange ratio and the relating quantities of final products which are traded depend almost entirely on the situation in the consumption sector. A possible effect of the law of non-proportional returns has no influence on this;
- the means of production are original, or at least quantitatively given and re-allocatable. There may be comparative cost differences, whereas in the realization of advantages which are present in the existence of these, the law of the non-proportional returns may play a part. For a correct solution of the problems of the optimum exchange ratio, the degree of production specialization and the volume of international trade, it is essential to incorporate the production and consumption sectors of the various countries into the assessment with a satisfactory adjustment to one another. The effect of the law of non-proportional returns forms an aspect of this;
- one of the two re-allocatable production is original and the other one derived. In this way capital formation can be theoretically raised as a problem; for example, capital is then interpreted as 'previously performed labour'. In this methodological assumption capital formation depends on the labour used in the investment sector.[6] In the final chapter of this study

6. We saw this already in: *Waardering van het economisch denken.* Pg. 110-121.

we shall investigate further the importance of retaining methodologically the possibility of this within the comparative cost theory in order to achieve a correct link with the theory of economic growth. It is now of importance that in this situation the law of non-proportional returns does not occur. This three-fold differentiation includes implicitly two objections against a theoretical explanation of the optimum exchange ratio exclusively based on the effect of the law of non-proportional returns. In the first place it can be observed that even in the single case where this law applies, the non-constant costs will be no more than an aspect of all the factors on which basis the optimum exchange ratio is founded. When exclusively non-constant costs are taken into account, a remarkable result is achieved which will be discussed with the aid of table 3 and graph 2.

Table 3. Comparative cost theory; non-constant costs.

		Costs	Values	Production	Trade	Consumption
		c_1:c_2	c_1:c_2	c_1:c_2	c_1:c_2	c_1:c_2
Country I	Autarchy	1:5	1:$\frac{1}{5}$	50:10	—	50:10
	Open economy	1:3	1:$\frac{1}{3}$	106:5	$-56+11\frac{2}{3}$	50:$16\frac{2}{3}$
Country II	Autarchy	1:1	1:1	25:25	—	25:25
	Open economy	1:3	1:$\frac{1}{3}$	19:$36\frac{2}{3}$	$+56-11\frac{2}{3}$	75:25

The figures provided agree with Harrod's example. Britain (country II) has a comparative cost advantage in the production of coal (c_2); abroad (country I) has a similar advantage in the production of wheat (c_1). The progress from autarchy to international equilibrium can be seen in table 3 and graph 2 as an exclusive effect of the law of non-proportional returns. The points *a* (country I) and *b* (country II) thereby represent the autarchic equilibrium situations; it is therefore assumed that the consumers require the final products in accordance with their value ratios based on the production costs. Subsequently a production specialization takes place in country I as indicated by *aa*1; the production specialization in country II is represented by *bb*1. The international trade of country I is subsequently described by *a*1 *e*, the one of country II by *b*1 *f*. The result is a change in the consumption of *a* to *e* (country I) and of *b* to *f* (country II); when the cost ratios have changed from *a* to *d*, or *b* to *c* respectively.

The result of all this can be interpreted as a new state of equilibrium. Two

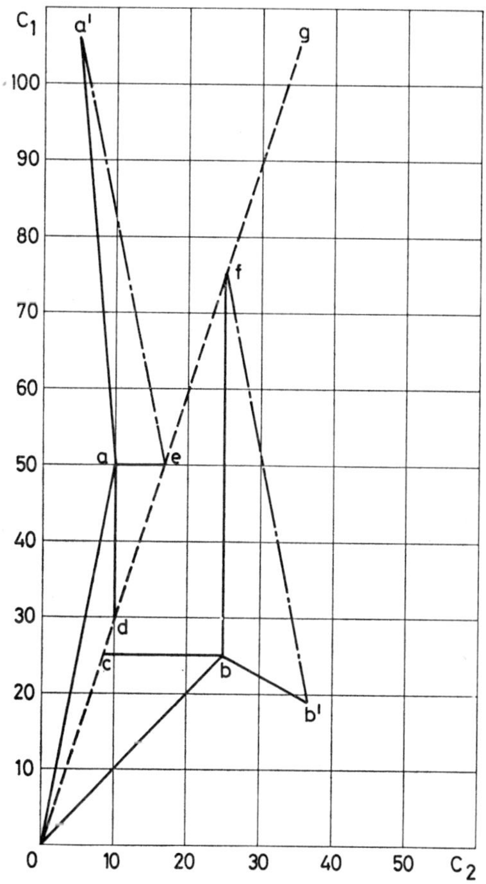

Fig. 2. Non-constant cost; comparative cost ratios.

things must be noted. In the first place it has been assumed in the consumption sector that it adjusts entirely in the demand for final products to the changed cost ratios. In fact, as with Ricardo, the consumption factor has been entirely ignored in this. As a result the above can only be an aspect of the comparative cost theory in general. If it is assumed that one can achieve with non-constant cost a comprehensive statement of the external exchange ratio the degree of production specialization and the volume of the international trade, then a – second – observation must be made, namely that the result of the analysis is only the description of a special case of comparative cost relations. Line 0*g* in graph 2 is not the indication of an optimum exchange ratio at comparative cost differences, but the reproduction of equal cost relations at the existence of non-constant costs after some production specialization and international trade.

Furthermore, a final statement of the optimum exchange ratio based on non-constant costs – also when thereby the consumption sector is more explicitly introduced than before – cuts off the way for a development of the comparative cost theory of given and re-allocatable production means – the above second possibility – towards an analysis with capital formation as a problem, which was called above the third possibility regarding the nature of the production factors. This is an undesirable methodological limitation, as it prevents a good connection of the comparative cost theory to the growth theory.

Based on the indicated reservations, non-constant costs will be excluded from this study, except when discussing the Heckscher/Ohlin theory.

II. COMPARATIVE COST THEORY AND LABOUR THEORY OF VALUE

The 'Principles' of Ricardo have caused a certain confusion in literature as a number of authors hold the opinion that in it the comparative cost theory – despite Ricardo's observations to the contrary – is based on the labour theory of value. Owing to this it is necessary to systematically investigate the comparative costs and the labour cost theory of value.

In addition, it remains an open question whether with the application of labour saving as the criterion for the result of international trade, the optimum external exchange ratio, the degree of production specialization and the quantities of final product to be traded can be correctly indicated. These two subjects will be dealt with in this chapter.

1. Labour as sole production factor

Haberler stresses in his 'Theory of international trade' that the law of comparative costs was little appreciated for a long time in Germany owing to its original relation with theory of labour value. Belief in this relationship is still active. 'Ricardo has based his theory (i.e. the comparative cost theory) on the labour cost theory of value' says Rose in an introduction to a collection of international-economic papers, published a few years ago.[1] In the Netherlands de Roos stated that 'the classical theory, the theory of comparative cost differences, was based on the labour cost theory of value'.[2] In an indirect way Enke and Salera support this opinion: 'The labour theory is undoubtedly the weakest part of the classical treatment of international trade'.[3] The interpretation of the classical theory by Graham points in the same direction. This author criticizes the 'equation of international demand' of Mill, which will be discussed later, and which shows some similarity with

1. Klaus Rose, *Theorie der internationalen Wirtschaftsbeziehungen*. Pg. 14.
2. F. de Roos, *Theorie van de internationale economische betrekkingen*. Pg. 116.
3. Stephen Enke & Virgil Salera, *International Economics*. Pg. 213.

Ricardian thought with regard to the adroitness of the market parties in the determination of the external exchange ratio. According to Graham, with the 'equation' the attention of the classics remained limited to the day to day market dealings. However, that is not sufficiently within the scope of the theory of international trade, as special attention must be paid to long term equilibrium prices. According to Graham the classics could not go this far 'Since the classical economist thought of the costs of production not in terms of opportunity cost but of labour costs of production and it was obvious that comparative labour could not be used to explain *international* values, they felt virtually forced to abandon cost in their international value theory'.[4]

This criticism points out that according to the classics the internal price structure is formed according to the rules of the labour cost theory of value, whereas in international dealings, their value is limited to the day to day market dealings, on which – as is known – costs have no influence. As will be shown below, this interpretation is inadequate. This also applies to the attempt by Viner to qualify the relationship between the comparative cost theory and the labour cost theory of value with the classical economists as incidental and without essential meaning: 'The association of the comparative cost doctrine with the labour cost theory of value is a historical accident, a result merely of the fact that Ricardo in his pioneer exposition of it, expressed real costs in terms of quantities of labour. Except for Ricardo, none of the classical expounders of the doctrine of comparative costs, with the relatively unimportant and partial exception of James Mill, was an exponent of the labour cost theory of value'.[5]

However, this ignores the fact that Ricardo's interpretation of the comparative cost doctrine particularly has had a great influence which is why there is still an unfulfilled need for a systematic explanation of the relationship between that doctrine and the Ricardian labour cost theory of value. Initially attention should be concentrated on the production sector, highlighting the question of where this principle must be placed in the comparative cost doctrine. It is recommended in the treatment of this subject that a distinction should be made between the situation:

- before opening the frontiers. Then Ricardo considers labour determines the cost ratios, whereas at the moment the 'opportunity costs' are fairly generally accepted for the purpose. The effect of this difference of opinion is the subject of this para;
- after opening the frontiers. When dealing with this we refer to the previous

4. Frank D. Graham, *The Theory of International Values*. Pg. 326.
5. Jacob Viner, *Studies in the Theory of International Trade*. Pg. 490.

chapter, when although it was apparent that Ricardo did not consider the labour cost theory of value applicable within the comparative cost doctrine, he did indicate the advantage of production specialization and international trade with labour saving. The extent to which it is possible to solve in this way the three fundamental questions – the optimum external exchange ratio, the degree of production specialization and the extent of international trade, will be dealt with in the next section.

'Opportunity costs' are considered to be the quantity c_1 which must be sacrificed in order to acquire a marginal unit c_2. It is usual to indicate graphically the production sector based on this concept by means of transformation curves.

Such a curve shows various combinations of final products, requiring the same production means for each combination. The question now is whether the Ricardian labour cost theory of value affords an opportunity to construct these lines. In answering it is essential – with the least possible philosophically biased considerations – to differentiate between the absolute and the relative labour cost theory of value. In the first case – approaching the problem from a marxist angle – labour is the sole source of value; it is the unique instrument with the aid of which man creates his life-environment. The sole thing, nothing can be compared with it, it is unique. Measurements and comparisons are excluded.

The construction of a transformation curve is then simply impossible. Absolute labour value in this sense is incorporated in the non-reproduceable final product; in the inimitable peak performance of a great artist. Economic thinking does not penetrate this area. For the economy labour can be performed by many and is repeatable in the course of time, so that the results of labour can always be compared. We then have a relative labour cost theory of value, which – according to Ricardo in agreement with Smith – means 'that all things became more or less valuable in proportion as more or less labour was bestowed on their production'.[6] With this interpretation, labour as an 'opportunity costs' factor determines the value ratios and there will be no conflict between the labour cost theory of value and the 'opportunity costs' theory. One may wonder whether the one has a greater real significance than the other. At this stage two points must be made. In the first place, the 'opportunity costs' without connection to the relative labour cost theory of value probably present a truer picture of reality than with that connection. Here some remarks by Haberler are interesting[7]; when – according to this

6. David Ricardo, *The Principles*. Pg. 7.
7. Gottfried von Haberler, *The Theory of International Trade*. Pg. 175 etc.

author exclusively – labour is applied as a homogeneous production factor, there are in principle no problems, as the labour costs are clearly the sole 'opportunity costs'. This is the case with Ricardo. However, this is an oversimplification. In reality labour is heterogeneous, and moreover other means of production must be applied as well. Consequently, the actual 'opportunity costs' include much more than homogeneous labour. Secondly, it is probable that influences from the consumption sector on the cost ratios will be accepted to an inadequate degree when connecting the 'opportunity costs' to the labour cost theory of value. Significantly, Cairnes talks about the 'normal price' as price in accordance with the relative labour cost theory of value: 'A reduction in the cost of producing a hat will lower its price, but will have no tendency to effect the price of another thing'.[8] As this chapter is limited to the production sector, we may ignore this aspect now.

On balance it means that Ricardo may have taken a correct, yet oversimplified cost concept as his starting point. We will now retain the simple presentation according to Ricardo, in order to avoid a tension between the 'opportunity costs' and the labour cost theory of value as long as the frontiers have not been opened. This opens the way for investigating the extent to which it is possible in the wake of Ricardo – and consequently with labour saving as criterion – to give an indication of the optimum external exchange relation, the degree of production specialization and the quantities to be traded.

2. Labour saving and exchange ratio

The reply to the question as to the extent labour saving as criterion in the comparative cost theory can withstand criticism, may be introduced with a general survey of the possibilities of finding an external exchange ratio. We assume that there are two countries which, before proceeding to product specialization and international trade, both have an economic equilibrium as indicated by point a in figure 3.[9] As these equilibrium positions are realized within a closed community they form a given starting point for the theory regarding the consequences of the international economic approach. When opening the frontiers the prosperity positions are subsequently functionally linked, more precisely, by the international trade which is decided. As to

8. J. E. Cairnes, *Some Leading Principles of Political Economy Newly Expounded.* Pg. 105.
9. See for the following examination our thesis *Economische orde en Europese monetaire integratie*. Pg. 3-5.

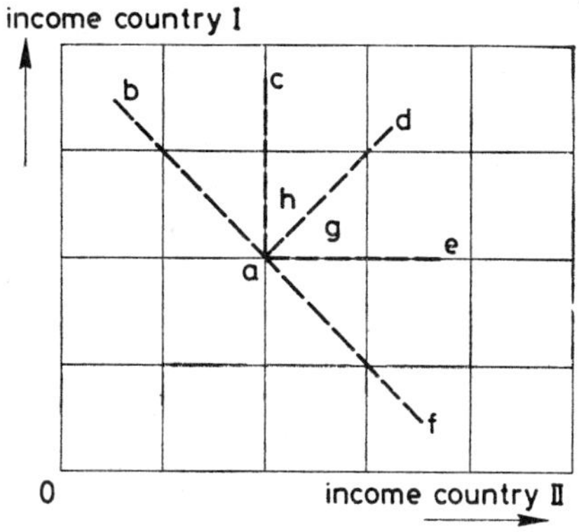

Fig. 3. International dependence of income positions.

the result of this, four different situations can be imagined. In the first place there is the possibility of absolute exploitation by one country regarding the other. This causes a reduction in the prosperity of one country. Figure 3 shows in the line section *a b* absolute exploitation of country II, line section *f* indicates absolute exploitation of country I. Subsequently, there may be a case of relative exploitation, when the prosperity of both countries increases, but the increase is relatively greater in one country. In the region *g* country I is relatively exploited, this is the case in *h* with country II. In the third place a limit can be drawn between absolute and relative exploitation. The prosperity position only improves in one country, whereas that of the other country remains constant. This is shown in figure 3 with the line sections *a c* and *a e*.

This general examination can now be consolidated to some extent. For this purpose table 4 – according to the labour coefficients immediately following figure 1 – distinguishes five exchange ratio when the result of the international trade is repeatedly expressed in a saving of labour units, these have been symbolized with *e*.

Table 4. Exchange ratios and labour saving.

$\overset{I}{\alpha}_{c_1} = 1; \overset{I}{\alpha}_{c_2} = 2; \overset{II}{\alpha}_{c_1} = 2; \overset{II}{\alpha}_{c_2} = 1.$

Exchange ratio		Labour seving Country I	Country II	Situation Fig. 2
1.	$c_1{:}3c_2$	$+5l$	$-1l$	*a b*
2.	$c_1{:}2c_2$	$+3l$	—	*a c*
3.	$c_1{:}c_2$	$+1l$	$+1l$	*a d*
4.	$2c_1{:}c_2$	—	$+3l$	*a e*
5.	$3c_1{:}c_2$	$-1l$	$+5l$	*a f*

As was the case in the last chapter, labour required in the home country for the production of the imported product has been compared to the labour used for the production of exports. For example, in the event of exchange ratio 2 country I receives $2c_2$ for which it must use in home production four labour units according to the labour coefficient; simultaneously one c_1 is released which has cost one labour unit, from which a saving of three labour units remains. In a business situation as depicted in table 4 exclusive exchange ratio 3 leads to an improvement in the prosperity of both countries. Can this be seen as an optimum external exchange ratio? At first sight one is inclined to say 'yes', yet difficulties arise when studying the problem further. In exchange ratio 3, each country saves one labour unit and that appears to be stable. However, we have no standard for placing the labour of different countries on one denominator and consequently cannot legitimately provide any decision regarding the equilibrium in the exchange ratio 3. Perhaps it may be necessary for the sake of equilibrium to exchange on the basis of $c_1 : 1\frac{1}{2}c_2$ or $1\frac{1}{2}c_1 : c_2$, also then a labour saving is achieved in both countries. We must conclude that so far a choice is impossible between all the possibilities with regard to the exchange ratio at which labour saving is achieved by each of the participating countries. The cause is apparent. The criterion of labour saving is limited to national frontiers and cannot be used comparatively with relation to the individual countries. After all, it is nothing more than a returns/cost comparison for each country individually with its own labour as a standard of value. This leads to the conclusion that with the combination of the immobility of the production factors between countries and using the labour saving as standard for the utilisation of advantages present in differences of cost ratio from country to country, Ricardo decided on an application of the absolute labour cost theory of value within the theory of comparative costs. The authors who have already indicated this are right. According to a second conclusion, it is in principle impossible to indicate the optimum external exchange ratio and consequently, the degree of production specialization, plus the extent of the international trade, based on the labour saving. The criterion of labour saving does not produce a scientific insight into the possible balanced relations for the production and consumption sectors of trading in mixed economic systems. Particularly from a methodological point of view, this conclusion is important. After all, it contains the fundamental question whether in the doctrine of comparative costs the countries are principally facing each other in a conflict situation, or endeavouring to combine together to achieve a simultaneous equilibrium in their production and consumption sectors. What are we doing? Is the subject of our study a doctrine of conflicts, in which one country will perpetually strive for improvement in its prosperity level at the expense of the other? In this case line *a d* in figure 3 expresses a power equilibrium; it will move to the advantage of the country which can relatively increase its power – in so far as this influences the external exchange ratio. In this case the subject of our study is an analysis of power relations in international trade. This is one possibility; the other one is that the object of the comparative cost doctrine consists of the description of an optimum relative prosperity, dealing with the problem of the extent to which the participating countries can improve their levels of prosperity with each others help. In this case line *a d* indicates a possible 'peace in order'; this is the situation in which neither of the participating countries considers it necessary from an economic point of view to introduce changes in the production specialization and international trade.

If labour value is decisive, the comparative cost doctrine forms a doctrine of conflicts; if an economic value concept as described in our 'Introduction' is assumed, it forms in principle an equilibrium analysis, which will be apparent later.

The study can be continued in a two-fold manner. In the first place, we could say that the labour saving may suffice as a criterion in the theory of international trade between communistic-centrally planned national economies.[10]

In this connection it is typical that a study of an East-German author, published some years ago, does not go beyond the conclusion that a production specialization and international trade may produce labour saving in comparative cost differences.[11]

However, we could go on to say that the labour saving criterion does not fit into the value concept which dominates our society and consequently we must use another standard. The result of this is a different approach which can no longer be compared to the comparative cost theory in the East and West. Naturally, it is desirable to avoid such a dichotomy. To this purpose, and this concerns the second possible reaction to the inadequacy of the Ricardian theory, we attempt a further analysis of the nature of labour saving as a criterion in the comparative cost doctrine. Perhaps it is possible, without reference to a fundamental difference in value concept, but based on a strictly logical analysis, to reach a viewpoint which enables us to correct the criterion

10. In which the exploitation also practically played an important part, see our study *Economische orde en Europese monetaire integratie*. Chapter I, para 2.
11. Gunther Kohlmey and other authors, *Nationale Produktivität, dynamische Produktionen, internationale Wirtschaft*. Pg. 88-91 and 150-161 resp.

used so far. In this way it may be shown that – besides the principle rejection in principle of the labour cost theory of value as a basis for the entire social economic situation – this theory does not provide good results within the comparative cost doctrine from a strictly theoretical point of view either. This is the case when the labour cost theory of value does not offer the possibility of providing a solution to the three fundamental problems of the theory of comparative costs. We shall follow this second approach; some preliminary work has in fact already been carried out.

In the previous chapter we established that Ricardo's theory was limited to the micro-economic indication of a technical production condition in order to proceed with mutual advantage to production specialization and international trade. The quantitative dimension of the means of production and the consumption sector were not included in the study. The above para established an addition to this with the introduction of the transformation curve, which implies that the quantitative dimension of production means is incorporated in the analysis. This was an unobtrusive concession to be made by the relative labour cost theory of value in order to reach agreement with the 'opportunity costs' theory. The continuation of the analysis requires the introduction of a new symbol:

L = the number of labour units (labour potential)

Subsequently, transformation curves can be designed with the data of table 5, as is shown in figure 4. The introduction of the transformation curve in this manner is an extension of the Ricardian theory, as in this way the production sectors are introduced in a macro-economic manner. At this stage Ricardo

Table 5. Specialization of production and international trade.

Situation	Country I - $\alpha c_1=1; \alpha c_2=2$ L=60				Country II - $\alpha c_1=2; \alpha c_2=1$ L=80					
	Production		Consumption		Production		Consumption		Trade	
	c_1	c_2	c_1	c_2	c_1	c_2	c_1	c_2	c_1	c_2
Autarchy	30	15	30	15	20	40	20	40	–	–
Open economy	60	–	30	30	5	70	35	40	30	30

did not proceed beyond a micro approach. For a correct model of the comparative cost doctrine it is essential to study closely the different micro and macro aspects. This has been done inadequately in a study by Shone, when describing transformation curves which are similar to the ones of figure 4. The graph concerned shows, according to Shone, 'the situation put forward by Ricardo and Torrens, namely country II being able to produce more of both goods than country I. In other words, country II has an absolute advantage in the production of both goods'.[12] This mixing of the transformation curve and the ratio of the absolute cost levels is open to criticism. The transformation curve as a macro concept includes an indication of the quantities of final product which can be produced; it depends on the quantities and the technical suitability of the production means. The ratio of the absolute cost levels – micro economically – is apparent from a comparison of the returns per unit of production means. It was apparent, for example, in the last chapter, that in Ricardo's example Portugal can produce more wine and cloth per labour unit than Britain; owing to the higher productivity of each labour unit, Portugal had a lower absolute cost level. However, this is totally removed from the transformation curve and from the comparative cost doctrine. Going back to figure 4, we limit the examination in the first instance to the autarchic equilibria; these have been shown in figures in table 4 based on the data. In figure 4 they are indicated by points *A* and *B*. These have been combined in figure 3 and abstractly indicated by point *a*. The ratio in which

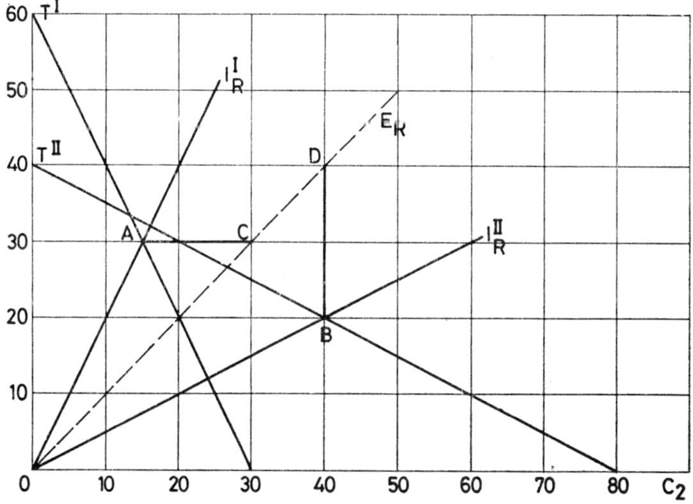

Fig. 4. Specialization of production and international trade.

12. R. Shone, *The Pure Theory of International Trade*. Pg. 16. Shone assumes a transformation curve of country II which is always higher than the one of country I.

the final products are demanded agrees in points *A* and *B* with those in which they are produced.

The effect of this will be further examined at a later stage, with among other things, the introduction of indifference curves. The problem we are interested in at the moment is the actual progress with specialization and international trade from the autarchic equilibria. The conditions of the application of the comparative cost theory have thereby been met, as the cost ratios are different in the various countries and production factors can be re-allocated. Further to table 4 and without further investigation (which will follow later), we assume that the international trade takes place based on an exchange ratio $c_1 : c_2$. Country I reduces the production of c_2 and concentrates entirely on c_1, of which at complete specialization, 60 units are produced. Subsequently, $30c_1$ is exported against an import of $30c_2$. Simultaneously country II – although not entirely – specializes on the production of c_2, of which, in exchange for $30c_1$, thirty units are exported. The result of this is important. Two points are worthy of note. In the first place, production specialization and international trade are a simultaneous process, causing in both countries a net increase of the final product which is relatively most expensive for them to produce. It is therefore this increase of final products, which is the real advantage of production specialization and international trade and not – and this concerns the second noteworthy point – the labour saving. In fact there is no labour saving at all; with regard to this production factor, it can only be established that re-allocation takes place. This implies two things. In the first place the criterion used so far is no longer applicable, as in reality no labour saving occurs. No results can be achieved when it is intended to analyse theoretically the advantages in the comparative costs using the labour cost theory of value. The Ricardian comparative cost doctrine only includes one – admittedly correct – production technical condition, plus labour as sole production factor, which does not move between countries as data; these are inadequate for a theoretical analysis of production specialization and international trade to provide an answer to the fundamental questions involved. At the time de Jong correctly concluded that the doctrine of comparative costs has indeed been formed historically from the labour cost theory of value, however, there is no logical connection between the two – in the sense that the first should support the second.[13] The lack in this connection can be shown even more clearly by our conclusion that the comparative cost doctrine will not reach the required development if based on the labour cost theory of value. Secondly, it is not necessary to investigate

13. A. M. de Jong, *Internationale handel en handelspolitiek*. Pg. 16-17.

based on the actual advantage – consequently, the net increase of final products as described above – how to solve the three questions for optimum exchange ratio, degree of production specialization and the size of the international trade. Naturally, the consumption sector will play an important part.

III. ANALYSIS VIEWED FROM THE CONSUMPTION SECTOR

The Ricardian approach invites a search for the precise location of the optimum external exchange ratio between the I_R curves, in order to be able to answer the essential questions of the comparative cost theory. The manner of approach as described in Ricardo's 'Principles' – characterized by an incomplete choice of data and consequently methodologically inadequate – proved unsuitable for achieving this objective. A broader view is essential. This is why in the works of Mill, Marshall and Edgeworth where the analysis are now popular not undertaken from the production sector, but rather pointedly from the consumption sector.

1. Mill and Marshall

John Stuart Mill closely follows Ricardo. In the existence of comparative cost differences the various countries have the opportunity of specializing in their production and subsequently moving to international trade based on an external exchange ratio which must be between the I_R-lines. It is necessary to explore further the effect of the internal exchange ratio lines as drawn in figures 1 and 4.

All that has been said about the curves so far is that an equal amount of labour has been applied at each point on them to the production of c_1 and c_2 respectively, whereas the coincidence of the I_R-lines indicates the existence of equal cost ratios in the individual countries. This implies that the I_R-curves represent the internal cost relations; they are a clear representation of the value of c_1, expressed in c_2. So long as labour is exclusively a scarce production factor, the I_R-curves can be called without objection, Ricardian value ratio lines. This is indicated by Mill in his discussion of international trade: 'Suppose that in England 10 yards of broadcloth cost as much labour as 15 yards of linen, and in Germany as much as 20'.[1] This indication of

1. J. S. Mill, *Principles of Political Economy*. Pg. 352 etc.

comparative cost differences via the value of the final products has a Ricardian flavour. However, this starting point, and as much the production sector, is ignored by Mill when a new element enters the study, which is only from then on one of real importance. This concerns a deviation from 'the natural price', which was described already by Adam Smith as the 'higgling of the market'. In this connection it must be said that Smith's thinking is a continuous balancing of idealism and reality: 'On the one hand inductive research, on the other aprioristic speculation, based on the "natural" hypothesis'.[2]

This dual mode of thinking especially applies to the price theory in the 'Wealth of Nations', which is fairly clearly described by Gray: 'The natural price is in its nature an ideal; opposite to it is the actual or market price which is arrived by conditions of demand and supply and the competition among buyers and sellers'.[3] This theoretical price dualism is important in this instance, because Mill transfers it to the theory of international trade. In addition to the above example of national cost ratios in Britain and Germany, he supposes a 'market price' at which '10 yards of cloth in both countries exchange for 17 yards of linen'. This implies that in Britain the 'higgling of the market' is expressed in a market price for cloth above the 'natural price'; in Germany this is the case for the market price for linen. But at these price ratios – states Mill, without further evidence, based on given supplies – not all cloth will be sold in Germany and Britain will have linen left over.

From this point onward the 'natural price' vanishes with Mill, and the study proceeds to search for a solution for the unsold goods. International trade is obvious in this respect. With some searching the countries will probably find an exchange ratio in order to realize what Mill calls 'the equation of international demand'. According to a description by de Roos, this concept means that 'the value of the demand of country *A* for the product of country *B* is equal to the value of the demand of country *B* for the product of country *A*'.[4] The 'equation' refers to equilibrium on the international scales. But it also means, in as far as it concerns Mill's line of thought, that this does not concern more than the clearing of the short term market in which the production sector and the costs no longer play an essential part. In this way, as will be again stressed later – Mill places his analysis entirely in the consumptive sector.

2. John Kells Ingram, *Geschichte der Volkswirtschaftslehre*. Pg. 125.
3. Alexander Gray, *The Development of Economic Doctrine*. Pg. 132.
4. F. de Roos, *Theorie van de internationale economische betrekkingen*. Pg. 128.

Marshall has provided an explanation with the 'reciprocal demand curves'.[5] The effect is that Say's law – each supply creates its own demand – is introduced into international economy. After all, Marshall himself states: '"supply and demand" is but another expression for "reciprocal demand"'.[6] Supply and demand reciprocally recognize each other. In a graphical representation of this, and in accordance with a formulation by Towle, curves with 'the demands of the two countries for each other's products in terms of their own products'[7] are formed. This description means that the 'reciprocal demand curve (*rd*) is an internal home exchange ratio line based on subjective assessment. Figure 5 shows the '*rd*' curves developed in connection with the pre-

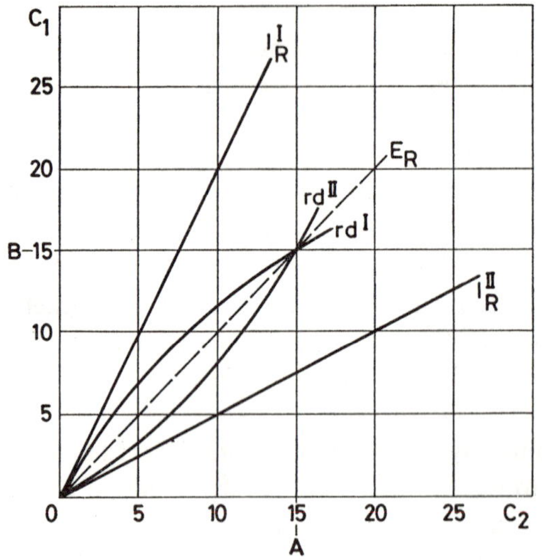

Fig. 5. Equation of international demand.

vious chapter. But now the subjective evaluations of the final products also play a part. Consequently, the I_R-lines also indicate the ratio in which the products are demanded by the consumers before the opening of the frontiers. They are a representation of the final product ratio according to the relative labour cost theory of value and also form the continued beginning of the '*rd*' curves, which are an indication of subjective assessment.

The first impression is that the '*rd*' curves provide a solution for the

5. Alfred Marshall, *The Pure Theory of Foreign Trade. The Pure Theory of Domestic Values.* Pg. 6 etc.
6. Alfred Marshall, *Money, credit and commerce.* Pg. 160.
7. Lawrence W. Towle, *International Trade and Commercial Policy.* Pg. 94.

problem as described at the end of the last chapter. The actual advantage, which can be achieved in the existence of comparative cost differences by production specialization and international trade is a net increase of the final product which is produced by a country with relatively high costs, as was pointed out there. In order to provide a precise description of this, the comparative cost theory – assuming autarchic equilibrium situations and, in addition, open frontiers – must provide the answers concerning the location of the external exchange curve, the degree of production specialization and the size of the international trade. Examining figure 5, it appears as if the '*rd*' curves satisfactorily answer these questions. After all, line sections $0A$ and $0B$ can be interpreted as net increase of c_2 in country I and of c_1 in country II respectively. And subsequently, the '*rd*' curves, based on subjective assessment, when c_1 in country II has a net increase, whereas this is the case in country I for c_2, are a correct representation of the two laws of Gossen. Based on these considerations, in which obviously the 'equation of international demand' is realized, the point of intersection of the '*rd*' curves can be considered as determining the location of the external exchange ratio. In accordance with that point $15c_1$ and $15c_2$ are traded.

Some critical observations must be made regarding this theory. It is remarkable that in the manner of approach of Mill and Marshall the consumption sector is presented entirely independently. The analysis starts with the determination of a 'higgling of the market'; from that point onwards there is no longer any connection with the production sector. It is not known therefore whether the international exchange as indicated by figure 5 is caused by the endeavour to achieve the advantages of comparative cost differences. Perhaps international trade has an entirely different cause. Because of this the representation on figure 5 can no longer be accepted indiscriminately as an explanation of the external exchange relation at comparative cost differences. A more clearly defined treatment of the relationships between production and consumption is essential. This is of fundamental importance in the construction of a theoretical model of international trade.

The question remains whether Mill and Marshall have indeed placed the 'equation of international demand' and the '*rd*-curves' within the scope of the comparative cost theory of Ricardo, who claimed to have relinquished the labour cost theory within the theory of comparative costs. However, it later became apparent that within the Ricardian comparative cost theory, the absolute labour cost theory is applied. At the beginning of this chapter it became apparent that Mill tried with the 'equation' to provide an explanation for the optimum external exchange ratio at comparative cost differences. The question now remains whether Mill and Marshall in the concrete solution of this subject indeed used comparative cost differences – plus the production specialization emerging from this and international trade – as a basis. We shall first concentrate on Mill and at the end of the next para we shall further investigate Marshall's line of thought.

In Mills' analysis there is no relation between 'equation of international demand' and the comparative cost theory. International trade – within the scope of which the 'equation' is realized – only commences according to the 'Principles' of Mill when there is a 'higgling of the market'. At that moment the presentation of the final products has been made. This constitutes a fundamental difference with the comparative cost theory, as in the latter this presentation is not determined a priori; in the contrary, it will be subjected to great changes owing to production specialization.

However, this does not mean that the concept of the 'equation' is limited to the provision of a statement of price formation by the day by day market dealings and the passage of this across the frontiers. However, this opinion is held by Graham as was apparent in the last chapter. Yet, the 'equation', in a much more general way than in Graham's theory, points in the direction of international trade, in which the costs but not the cost ratios play a part. In the search for the autarchic equilibrium as the basic point for the theory of international trade, the question remains whether the theory of comparative costs – and within the framework of that doctrine, the introduction of demand factors – suffices even in principle. Do the comparative cost differences, to which Mill tried without success to connect the 'equation of international demand' – form the exclusive foundation for the theory of international trade? The comparative cost theory implies methodologically the possibility of the differentiated application of production means, but this is frequently not so. It is therefore impossible to explain with this theory the advantage to be gained by the Netherlands through the export of tulip bulbs and the import of cigarettes. The tulip field is not suitable for growing tobacco. For the sake of a data description, which is realistic, it is necessary to observe that in many cases the means of production cannot be applied in different ways. If reality is not adequately observed in this respect, the result will be a theory of international trade which is nothing more than a 'system of statements' without empirical meaning. As long as the equation is considered to be following the Ricardian theory by the introduction of demand factors and as such to be the key-stone of the comparative cost theory, the impossibility of differentiated application of production means is not examined. However, a methodologically sound model of the entire international economy requires a differentiation between, on the one hand, international trade without the possibility of re-allocating production means and in which the comparative cost theory does not apply and, on the other hand, international trade with the possibility of re-allocation and in which trade across the frontiers is inspired by the existence of comparative cost differences. In the light of this the study by Edgeworth is especially interesting.

2. Edgeworth

Initially, the leader of the Cambridge-school after Marshall, appears to add little in his discussion of 'international trade'[8] to the 'equation of international demand'. Edgeworth is somewhat clearer than Marshall in explaining the supposed relationship between the comparative cost theory and the '*rd*' curves; he places these curves for the first time with the I_R-lines in one graph, as shown in figure 5. This is important in so far as it shows the effort made by Edgeworth to provide both the production and the consumption sector with a stable footing in the 'reciprocal demand' analysis. However, this is only a weak attempt to synthesize; after all the I_R-lines and the '*rd*' curves – drawn in accordance with Edgeworth's theory – take right from the beginning a different path, without touching or intersecting one another. Away from the origin, they have no further connection; even graphically production and consumption are separated. This issue will be further highlighted after the construction of 'trade indifference curves' in chapter VI.

At a later stage Edgeworth examines the equilibrium between two countries trading with each other, when country I exports two products and country II one product. Not the fact that this concerns three products, instead of the usual two, makes the relative pages in the 'Papers' so interesting, but it is more important that Edgeworth with complete production functions allots far more significance to the objective value aspect than was the case with Mill and Marshall.

The analysis of Edgeworth is mainly algebraic and rather complicated. The author has made little effort to put his thoughts clearly on paper. This makes it understandable but none the less regrettable, that Edgeworth's contribution, which is now becoming popular, has remained practically unknown. We shall provide a verbal report and a graphical explanation of the principle thoughts.

8. F. J. Edgeworth, *Papers Relating to Political Economy*. Vol. II pg. 3 etc.

The production functions cover the fact that in country I the goods x and y – which we combine to c_1 – are produced, whereas country II exclusively produces the product z – which will be indicated here as c_2. In addition, Edgeworth only takes into account labour as a scarce production factor. The volumes of the final products – given the labour coefficients – are determined with full employment as the starting point. These are graphically shown in figure 6 by points A (country I) and B (country II); these are the autarchic starting points. A line directly connecting points A and B results in a commercial substitution curve, the meaning of which will become apparent. The autarchic starting point provides an important difference with the theory of Mill and Marshall, as no claim is made about the 'higgling of the market'. The fact that country I in the initial situation has only c_1, and country II only c_2, is the result of the nature of the production functions.

The consumer pattern as described by Edgeworth in his 'Papers', can here be indicated by $\delta c_2 = \mu \delta c_1$. In this δ is naturally delta (small change), whereas μ represents the subjective marginal substitution rate of c_1 in c_2.

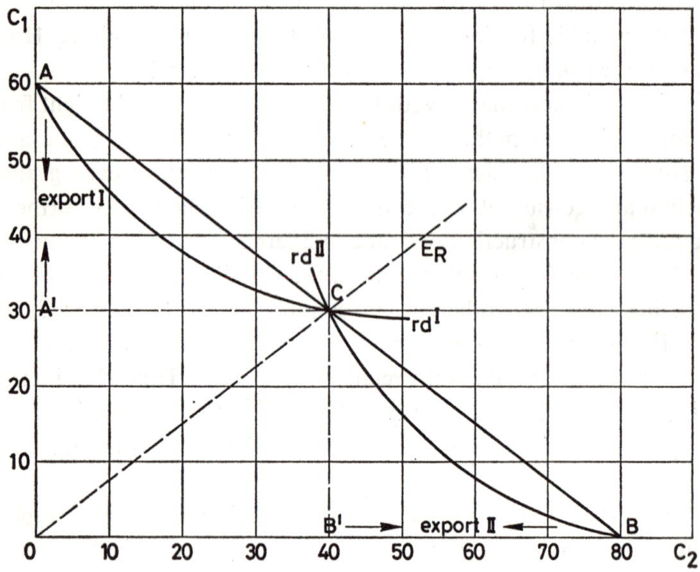

Fig. 6. Reciprocal demand and specialization of production.

In fact, the '*rd*' curves have been defined in this manner; these have been included in figure 6. These curves, though not constructed by Edgeworth in the manner described, but which are a reliable graphical representation of his algebraic approximation, have with this indication a different path than those of Marshall, without any difference in meaning. This is because they do not start from the origin, but from the convex lines from point *A* for country I and from point *B* for country II. The path of the curve as indicated in figure 6, is obvious. When in the initial situation country I has exclusively c_1, it will be prepared to part with much c_1 for one unit of c_2. However, this willingness gradually diminishes with the decrease of c_1 and the increase of c_2. In country II the situation has been similarly calculated from c_2.

What remained obscure in the previous para is now obvious. Whereas Marshall drew the '*rd*' curves from the origin, owing to which the events in the production sector were not revealed, Edgeworth's theory, with an explicit consideration of the production sector, is inclined to draw these curves from the points *A* and *B*. Characteristic for *C* as the international point of equilibrium is that entirely in accordance with the 'reciprocal demand' theory, the marginal utility ratio is equal in both countries.

Following the above paragraph, we can further investigate to what extent Marshall's theory regarding the '*rd*' curves fits in with the comparative cost theory. Marshall has illustrated his line of thought with a figure example[9] which has become famous and is frequently quoted in the literature by people such as de Roos[10], Harris[11], and von Haberler.[12] It has been partially copied in table 6 with some additions – always underlined – for reasons of completeness.

The core of this example is in columns (1), (3), and (5). It is possible to introduce these in a graphical representation, with on the x-axis goods c_2, or the *E*-bales respectively, and on the y-axis goods c_1, or the *G*-bales respectively. Columns (1) and (5) contain the '*rd*' curve for country I, if one places the *E*-bales of column (1) with the corresponding *G*-bales of column (5) in a graph, then there is a curve which is analogous to the '*rd*' I-curve in figure 5. In a similar way is it possible to construct a curve analogous to the '*rd*' II-line in figure 5 commencing from the columns (1) and (2). This means that the diagram can serve to represent a process of international trade from the autarchic situation in period 0 to the international equilibrium in period 4.

However, a supposition must be included regarding the exchange ratio from period to period; for this purpose the 'reciprocal demand' of country I

9. Alfred Marshall, *Money, Credit and Commerce*. Pg. 162.
10. F. de Roos, *Theorie van de internationale economische betrekkingen*. Pg. 130.
11. Seymour E. Harris, *International and Interregional Economics*. Pg. 149.
12. G. von Haberler, *The Theory of International Trade*. Pg. 151.

has been chosen. Consequently, column (1) represents the export of c_2-goods ('*B*-bales') of Britain and columns (5) the c_1-goods export ('*G*-bales') from Germany. The effect of the entire issue now becomes clear. Without any change in the production sector, a specialized direction has been produced even before the frontiers are opened – international trade is achieved with reciprocal advantage.

Table 6. Marshall's figure on *rd*-curves.

	Schedule of terms on which *E* is willing to trade			Schedule of terms on which *G* is willing to trade			
Period	No. of *E*-bales	No. of *G*-bales per 100 *E*-bales at which *E* will buy those in (1)	Total of *G*-bales which *E* is willing to give for those in (1)	No. of *G*-bales per 100 *E*-bales at which *G* will buy those in (1)	Total no. of *G*-bales which *G* is willing to give for those in (1)	Consumption England *E*-bales	Consumption German *G*-bales
	(1)	(2)	(3)	(4)	(5)	(6)	(7)
0	–	–	–	–	–	180.000	144.400
1	10.000	10	1.000	230	23.000	170.000	121.400
2	30.000	30	9.000	143	42.900	150.000	101.500
3	60.000	46	27.600	95	57.000	120.000	87.400
4	90.000	78	70.200	78	70.200	90.000	70.200

Interpretation:
G = Germany – country I
E = England – country II
G – bale = c_1
E – bale = c_2

With this interpretation the diagram of Marshall leads to the same result as the observations by Mill and Edgeworth. They constitute three variations on one theme in the sense that the analysis starts with an already specialized production. Within the scope of the comparative cost theory this is methodologically not without criticism. After all, in that case both products will already be produced in the autarchic situation. A choice is now essential. Either the possibility of re-allocating the production means is absent, but then the comparative cost theory does not apply, or the production functions at comparative cost differences already include a complete specialization at the beginning of the analysis. However, this would not be a case of sure analysis, when a complete specialization is assumed, whereas in fact its occurrence or non-occurrence must be explained. Methodologically only the first interpretation is acceptable. We will extend on this in the next chapter.

All this establishes the fact that the statement of the external exchange ratio within the scope of the comparative cost theory of Mill, Marshall and Edgeworth is inadequate. Yet, especially in the 'reciprocal demand' described above, this is accepted on a large scale. In the Netherlands it is accepted by de Roos[13] and Wemelsfelder.[14] Implicitly, the 'equation of international demand' as an explanation of the comparative cost theory is included in the diagram provided by Janssen.[15] Benham provides an extensive theory about the comparative cost theory and further explains the location of the curve representing the exchange ratio, but whilst referring back to the 'equation'.[16] Haberler deals extensively with the same idea in a study of 'supply and demand in international trade'.[17] The 'reciprocal demand' idea with the above effect is stated and accepted in a work by Kemp.[18] All this is only a limited choice. A more detailed approach, in particular concerning the cooperation between production and consumption is overdue. An attempt to achieve this is the subject of our final chapter.

13. F. de Roos, *Theorie van de internationale economische betrekkingen*. Pg. 129-139.
14. J. Wemelsfelder, *Internationale economische betrekkingen*. Pg. 351.
15. L. H. Janssen, *Free Trade, Protection and Customs Union*. Pg. 9-14.
16. F. Benham, *The Terms of Trade*.
17. G. von Haberler, *The Theory of International Trade*. Pg. 145 etc.
18. M. C. Kemp, *The Pure Theory of International Trade*. Pg. 44.

IV. SUBSTITUTION OF FINAL PRODUCTS

The considerations in the last chapter led to the conclusion that it is useful to differentiate between international trade without the possibility of re-allocating production means and the situation when their re-allocation is possible. So far the general assumption was that the data selected for this differentiation should correspond as closely as possible to reality, so that the theory of international trade does not become a 'system of assertions' without any empirical meaning. From a methodological point of view, the difference is of practical importance, as in the various situations there is a different solution to fundamental problems regarding the optimum external exchange relation, the degree of production specialization and the size of international trade. This chapter deals with the search for a solution to these three questions in the event of absence of re-allocation.

1. Equal price ratios

A great merit of Edgeworth's analysis is that it provides a clear connection between production and consumption in international trade, without amendment in the application of production means. This chapter aims at a further extension of this line of thought. In addition to earlier examples and graphical representations, the study is in the first instance based on table 7. In period 0 the situation is equal to the autarchic initial points *A* and *B* in figure 6. Subsequently, attention is drawn to figure 7, and in 7a the '*rd*' curves have been drawn in accordance with the Marshall theory. In this original version they do not provide an insight into the adjustment process from autarchy to international equilibrium; but this was already apparent from the last chapter. The example of Marshall could only be interpreted there as the reproduction of a process of international trade from autarchic situations to international equilibrium based on a complementary hypothesis. This meant that from period 0 to period 4 trade took place on the basis

Table 7. International trade by substitution of final products.

Period	Consumption Country I		Consumption Country II		Trade	
	c_1	c_2	c_1	c_2	c_1	c_2
0	60	—	—	80	—	—
1	52½	10	7½	70	7½	10
2	45	20	15	60	15	20
3	37½	30	22½	50	22½	30
4	30	40	30	40	30	40

of the 'reciprocal demand' of country I. This representation need no longer be maintained. The earlier hypothesis is replaced by the initial point that during the entire process from autarchy to international equilibrium, trade occurs across the frontiers, in accordance with the ratio as shown by line *0C* in figure 7a and the data in the right column of table 7. The E_R-curve concerned represents an exchange ratio which enables simultaneous equilibrium in the various countries. Further evidence of this is provided in chapter V, para 2.

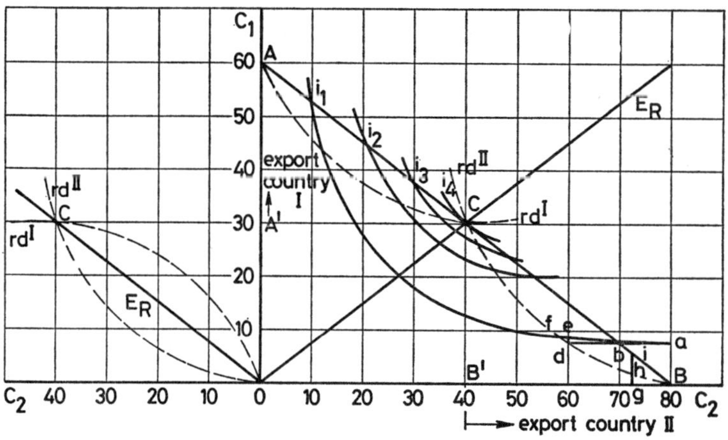

Fig.7a/7b. Substitution of final products at equal price ratios.

The '*rd*' curves according to the method of Marshall in figure 7a – of permanent analytical importance indicating the international equilibrium, as will become clear – have been drawn in accordance with Edgeworth's line of thought, in 7b. Additionally, line *AB* in the graph is already known from the last chapter as the commercial substitution curve. It represents the changes in the quantities of final production for each period, if this progresses on the basis of the exchange ratio already indicated. In the equilibrium situation a final production substitution has taken place for country I from *A* to *C* and for country II from *B* to *C*.

Subsequently, it was considered necessary to pay attention to an important difference between the situation where the means of production cannot be re-allocated and, on the other hand, the situation where possibilities of re-allocation exist. In this second case, the comparative cost theory applies; then production specialization and international trade lead to a net increase of the final product which was produced by the country concerned under the relatively least favourable circumstances possible before the frontiers were opened. This conclusion, at the end of Chapter II, will be further considered later from the point of view to what extent production specialization and international trade can result in an improvement of the satisfaction of consumer demand.

Owing to the absence of possibilities for re-allocation, the situation is entirely different in this chapter. Naturally, there is now no net increase of a specific final product. Production specialization is by definition excluded and international trade has only substitution of final products as a result. How effective is this type of trade across the frontiers? Again the satisfaction of consumer demand in the individual countries must show the benefits of international trade. For this reason indifference curves have been shown in figure 7b. These offer the possibility of a more precise introduction of the subjective value aspect as compared to the previous chapter.

The indifference curve has been defined as a line representing two consumption commodities in ever differing quantities and in which the utility of each combination is equal. Stonier and Hague note three peculiarities about this curve.[1] Owing to the positive marginal utility of each commodity its path is sloping downwards from left to right. Additionally, they cannot intersect, as then – contrary to elementary economic logic – the same combinations of final products would yield a different benefit. Finally, the indifference curve, under the influence of the changing marginal substitution ratio has a convex path in accordance with the laws of Gossen. This summary of properties is somewhat exaggerated. The third property – the convex path – after all implies the first one (sloping downwards from left to right). Additionally, the second is not one of the separate curve but of the curve relation. Consequently, only the convex path remains, so that Bailey quite correctly ob-

1. Alfred W. Stonier and Douglas C. Hague, *A Textbook of Economic Theory*. Chapter III, para 1.

serves: 'Beyond this, nothing can be said about the shape of an indifference curve without further assumptions about behaviour'.[2]

The theory of international trade as constructed by Mill, Marshall and Edgeworth, can be further developed by assuming a streamlined convex path, which is characteristic for a hyperbolic indifference curve. This has the property that the product of the co-ordinates is constant. Figure 7b shows four indifference curves of this nature. The location of the lines concerned depends on the absolute value of the product of the co-ordinates. Naturally, the curve will be higher when this value is greater. A higher level of satisfaction of consumer demand corresponds with this. Now the simultaneous arrival of a higher indifference curve in the different countries counts as a criterion for the volume of international trade. In that case there will be a simultaneous improvement in the satisfaction of consumer demand.

We shall now concentrate on a further explanation of the – assumed – actual events according to table 7 and figure 7. In period 0-1 the quantity c_1 in country II increases from *B* to *a* by $7\frac{1}{2}$ unit. At the same time, the quantity c_2 decrease in that country from *a* to *b*; that is by 10 units. At this point in the theory the essential meaning of the 'reciprocal demand' for the theory of international trade is more pronounced than in the previous chapter. In order to acquire a quantity c_1 of the size of *Ba*, country II is prepared to make available a quantity c_2 amounting to *ad*, which can be concluded from the nature of the '*rd*' curve. For this purpose the country concerned only has to relinquish a quantity c_2 amounting to *ab*. This means that the indifference curve passing through point *b*, guarantees a higher level of satisfaction of consumer demand than point *d* and consequently is located above this last point – namely in figure 7b at the level of *c*. Subsequently it intersects the '*rd*' curve at point *f*.

Line *AB* forms an expression of the substitution of the final products which takes place with this type of international trade; for the section indicated by *BC* it is the product curve for country II. Additionally, the '*rd*' curve is a cost line in the terminology of Von Wieser as 'lost benefit' and, limiting the study to the period 0-1, with an indication of the quantity *ad* of c_2, which can be relinquished in order to obtain *Ba* in c_1 based on the subjective value judgement of country II. The space between the commercial substitution line and the '*rd*' curve, which is indicated with the line section *db*, and assuming that subjective assessment – represents the advantage of international trade to country II in the period 0-1.

Figure 7b only shows the above graphically for country II in the period

2. Martin J. Baily, *National Income and the Price Level.* Pg. 94.

0-1; subsequent developments do not present many problems requiring explanation. It is important that over the periods the area between the commercial substitution curve and the '*rd*' lines becomes smaller. They intersect at point *C*, at the point where *AC* for country I and *BC* for country II touch the highest attainable indifference curve. Then *a, b, c, d, e* and *f* form together one point, namely the equilibrium for the two countries. This corresponds with the point of intersection of Marshall's method, which now clearly represents the international position of equilibrium. This can be explained a little further by a marginal-analytical manner of observation. The line of thought developed above presents favourable possibilities for this purpose, as after all, limiting the explanation to country II, each part of the '*rd*' II-curve, for example *Bh*, indicates marginal costs expressed in c_2, whereas when these costs are made, the line section *Bi* represents the corresponding marginal returns expressed in c_1. Naturally, the space between costs and returns decreases to the point of intersection of the '*rd*' line and the commercial substitution curve. Consequently point *C* indicates an equality of marginal costs and returns for the two countries. Beyond this point the marginal costs are in excess of the marginal returns as is the case when referring to both countries. In this way a marginal-analytical analysis realises to an optimum degree in point *c* the 'equation of international demand'. In figure 7 this takes place in a special manner as the price ratios in the two countries then become equal. After all, the reverse of the price ratio in an equilibrium situation is the marginal substitution ratio and these show uniformity in point *c*.

The international equilibrium in *C* is also interesting as a point from which changes in the exchange relations can be investigated. To this purpose, a technical improvement is assumed after the described equilibrium in period 4, by a decrease of αc_1 from 1 to 2/3. The consequences of this are shown in figure 8. A direct consequence of this is that the commercial substitution curve moves from *AB* to *EB*. Point *C* is the already established initial equilibrium as indicated in figure 7. The described structure of the consumption sectors with hyperbolic indifference curves, in reaction to the changes in the production sector of country I, now lead to the new equilibrium point *D*. It is remarkable that the product, which from period 4 is produced under relatively more favourable technical circumstances, proportionally decreases in price in both countries. In country II this decrease materialises through – for that country – an improved external exchange ratio. In period 4 this country only received $\frac{3}{4}c_1$ for c_2 (curve $E_R{}^4$); after the introduction of the technical improvement this is $1\frac{1}{8}c_1$ (curve $E_R{}^5$).

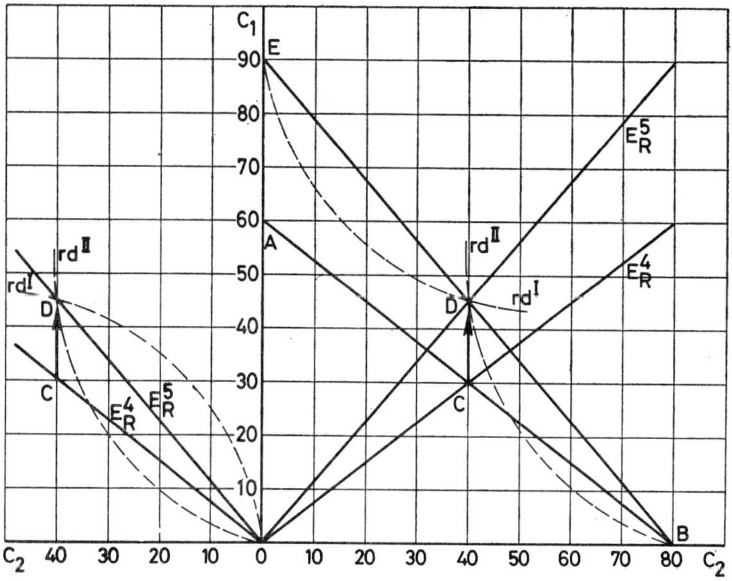

Fig. 8. Substitution of final products; equal price ratios and technical progress.

2. Unequal price ratios

The above para contains the details of a general theoretical description of international trade when the production means cannot be re-allocated. A dual starting point always applies. The one country – in our approach country I – only produces the consumption commodity c_1 and the other – country II – exclusively produces c_2. Consequently, there is initially in country I a relatively high assessment for c_2; in country II this is the case with regard to c_1. A construction of the '*rd*' curves in accordance with the method by Marshall, assumes this situation. When these curves are drawn from the point of origin they will intersect, according to Gossen's laws. Further to the example of Marshall, this point of intersection was chosen in such a way in the above paragraph, that when reaching international equilibrium, the price ratios in the different countries became equal.

The essential characteristic of the equilibrium analysis was that the lines indicating the final product substitution – when international trade takes place in accordance with the external ratio according to the point of intersection of the '*rd*' curves – touch with their terminal point the highest attainable indifference curve. The latter is at that point cut by the '*rd*' line. It is not essential that the price ratios in the different countries then become equal. This is indeed the case according to the example of Marshall, but this is a 'special case' of the general theory. In this paragraph this is further illustrated by the description of international trade by substitution of final products, when the price ratios do not become equal in the equilibrium situation. This will be the case when the indifference curves of the various countries are different and the external exchange ratio differs from the final product ratio according to curve *AB*. Such a situation is shown in figure 9. Now the independent influence of the consumption sector on the path of international trade is obvious. The commercial substitution curve *AB* is objective in nature, in such a way that its location is exclusively due to the conditions in the production sector. It is possible that it represents the actual substitution of the final products.

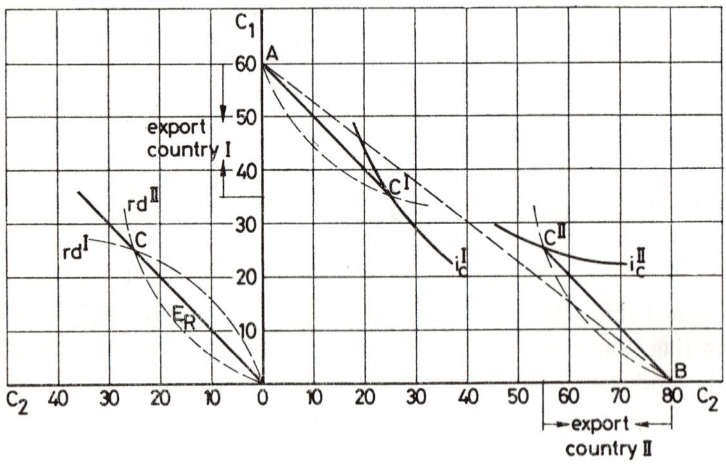

Fig. 9a/9b. Substitution of final products; unequal price ratios.

However, that is only the case in the situation of the last para. Matters are different in figure 9; there AC^{I} is the commercial substitution line for country I and BC^{II} for country II. Additionally, C^{I} and C^{II} represent the national equilibriums which are simultaneously reached by trade based on the external exchange relation *DC*. The marginal-analytical theory, as developed in the last para, remains completely intact.

Attention can now also be drawn to the consequences of technical progress; once again we assume that αc_1 decreases from 1 to 2/3. The consequence is shown in figure 10. What changes occur owing to the displacement of the curve *AB* to *EB*? The situation is analogous to the one shown in figure 8. In both cases it has been assumed that the '*rd*' curves move vertically. Once again this means a worsening of the exchange rate for country I. As a result the relative price decrease does not only occur in the producing country, it also occurs in country II.

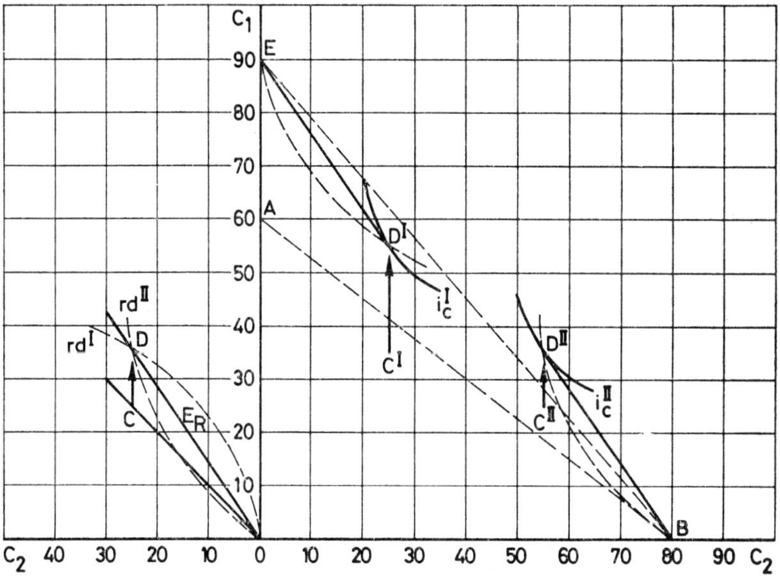

Fig. 10a/10b. Substitution of final products; unequal price ratios and technical progress.

Naturally, figure 10 only provides a specific manner of adjustment of the consumption sectors to the changed relations in production. However, the general picture is clear. A relatively large technical advance in a country where re-allocation of the means of production is not possible, leads to price decrease for the commodity concerned. This decrease will partially occur in the producing country, when the marginal substitution rate of the other commodity reduces simultaneously. Partially, there will be a price decrease abroad owing to the worsening of the exchange ratio. In the event of full employment and complete disposal of the final products, this will be relatively greater, when smaller in the home country.

In monocultures there are no re-allocation possibilities. The decrease of the labour coefficient indicated above is then expressed in favourable climatological circumstances, continued mechanisation and soil treatment, plant disease control, spraying, drainage, etc. The abstract picture of international trade can be given a greater validity by introducing these aspects. Under the influence of changing natural circumstances both large as well as small harvests are noted and commercial political measures – such as the international wheat, sugar and coffee agreements – are then no longer excluded from but contribute to the theoretical picture.

V. DIFFERENTIATED FACTOR RA

The second para of chapter I contains the following differentiation regarding the nature of production factors:

- they cannot be re-allocated and consequently, can only be used for the production of c_1 or c_2;
- they are original, at least quantitatively given and can be re-allocated;
- they are re-allocatable. And, assuming two production factors the one is original and the other derived.

This differentiation runs as a thread through our study. The first possibility appeared in chapters III and IV. International trade then resulted in substitution of final products. This chapter is concerned with the second possibility concerning the nature of the factors of production; the study continues from the end of chapter II.

1. The Heckscher/Ohlin principle

The theory of chapter II contains a simplification, as it does not go beyond labour being the original, quantitative datum and re-allocatable factor of production. When addditionally capital is introduced with the same characteristics, then the manner of approach of Heckscher and Ohlin becomes apparent. This is a macro-completion of the Ricardian micro theory. Ohlin's analysis, in his attempt 'to demonstrate that the theory of international trade is only a part of a general localization theory'[1], sees the economic process from a bird's eye point of view. Following Heckscher, he notices differences in the availability of the production means from region to region: 'In one region wheat must be produced by an intensive application of labour and capital on each little bit of land, in another, vast areas of land are barely used at all or cultivated with a very small amount of labour and capital'.[2]

1. Bertil Ohlin, *Interregional and International Trade*. Pg. XIII.
2. Id.; pg. 40.

These circumstances cause differences in price relations. In a country with a high capital/labour ratio, where capital is relatively easily available – products which are capital intensive will be relatively cheap to produce. On the other hand, labour intensive commodities will be relatively less expensive.

If this situation occurs in different ways in the various countries, then international trade will take place. Exchange across the frontiers can be seen as a substitute for the limited mobility of the production means. That is the heart of the Heckscher/Ohlin principle, which means that international trade occurs because of differences in the relative availability of the means of production. Naturally, this principle only applies to the original, at least given production means, as – if one of them is derived – the factor ratio may change. As – to be more precise – capital formation depends on the method by which labour is allocated, then the capital/labour ratio is theoretically no longer given. Then the Heckscher/Ohlin principle has implicitly lost its validity.

The relationship between the Ricardian theory and the Heckscher/Ohlin principle – the point we had just reached in our study – can be shown as based on the production functions (1) and (2), when the symbols written with capital letters always relate to macro magnitudes. Additionally

$$(1)\quad \alpha\, c_1 C_1 + \alpha\, c_2 C_2 = L$$
$$(2)\quad \varkappa\, c_1 C_1 + \varkappa c_2 C_2 = K$$
$$\varkappa = \text{capital coefficient}$$
$$K = \text{stock of capital goods}$$

In this the capital coefficient is a fraction within the numerator, the capital required for the production of the final product stated in the denominator. The sectorial indication occurs also now with the suffix c_1 or c_2 respectively.

Based on the production functions (1) and (2) the Theory of Ricardo and the Heckscher/Ohlin principle are numerically compared in table 8. It was taken into consideration that the Ricardian manner of assessment was limited to labour as a production factor, whereas this was not introduced as a macro magnitude.

The values indicated for L in 'Ricardo' form an addition by us. In Heckscher and Ohlin both labour and capital are macro magnitudes, which occupy a central place in the theory. Thus, differentiated factor relations can be seen as an important additional cause for the existence of comparative cost differences. Two points must be made in conjunction with table 8.

In the first place the table concerned contains a special situation, as the coefficients have precisely such a value in the production functions that the

Table 8. Ricardo and the Heckscher/Ohlin principle.

	αc_1	αc_2	L	$\varkappa c_1$	$\varkappa c_2$	K	$\frac{K}{L}$	c_1	c_2
Ricardo									
country I	1	2	60	–	–	–	–	30	15
country II	2	1	80	–	–	–	–	20	40
Heckscher/Ohlin									
country I	½	1	30	¼	½	15	½	30	15
country II	½	¼	20	1	½	40	2	20	40

transformation lines for labour and capital coincide. Naturally, this is a unique case. However, the coefficients concerned have only been chosen for reasons of simplicity in order to enable – in this para – a discussion of the concave transformation curve. The study will lead to the conclusion that this curve can be allotted only a very modest place in the comparative cost theory. It is not of essential importance in answering questions regarding the optimum exchange ratio, production specialization and the size of international trade. When, later on, capital formation is seen as a problem, the particular suppositions regarding production functions of table 8 are necessarily cancelled. Consequently, they have only an appropriate and not an essential meaning for the theory developed in this study.

Secondly, it is quite true that the production functions, even when the examination is limited to the autarchic situation, do not provide a solution regarding the ratio in which the final products are going to be produced. This requires the introduction of the consumption sector, which has been done in figure 11 – immediately following table 8 – with the already known hyperbolic indifference curve. As a result of this, point A (country I) and B (country II) form the autarchic equilibria on the point of intersection of the internal exchange ratio and transformation lines. With the indication of these equilibria in the manner shown, the micro theory regarding the technical production conditions for the existence of comparative cost differences according to Ricardo, and the closely connected macro approach regarding the differentiations in the factor ratios in accordance with Heckscher and Ohlin fit into the analysis. After all, the path of the transformation curves T^{I} and T^{II} in figure 11 is based on different production techniques and differentiated factor ratios in both countries. However, this is not the only positive aspect of the points A and B in figure 11. In addition the example provides a reply based on the normal economic value concept to the three

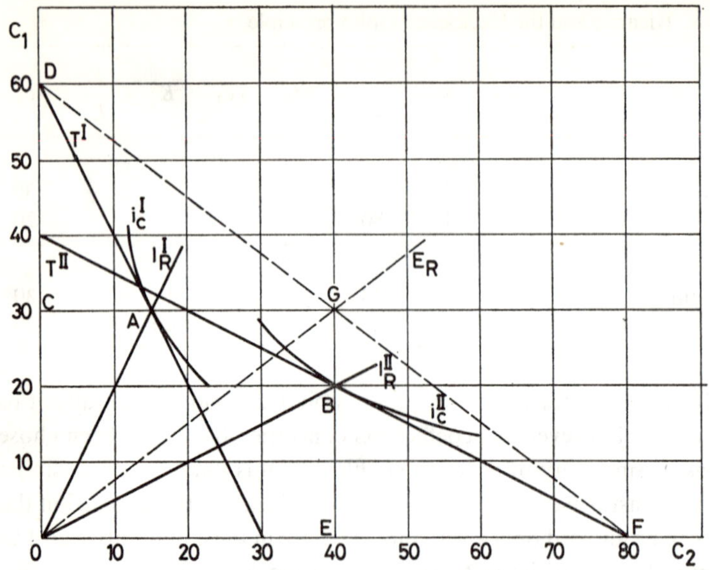

Fig. 11. International trade with full specialization of production.

fundamental questions of the comparative cost theory. With this second point an essential requirement of our study has been met because – when after the determination of the autarchic equilibria the frontiers are opened – the question arises once again for the optimum exchange ratio, the degree of production specialization and the volume of international trade.

Based on the Heckscher/Ohlin principle, the literature has provided a dual answer to these questions. We will provide a brief assessment.

The first reply covers the situation as indicated in figure 11, concerning countries of approximately equal size with rectilinear transformation curves. When countries proceed from the autarchic equilibrium situation to complete production specialization and that international trade which achieves equal final product relations, the export of country I amounts to a quantity c_1 amounting to *CD*, whilst country II exports to *EF* in c_2. Complete specialization and equal division subsequently form the basis for the international equilibrium in point *G*.

Methodologically this approach, which we find with Rose[3] and Schouten[4] can be attacked. It falls short because complete production specialization

3. Klaus Rose, *Theorie der Aussenwirtschaft*. Pg. 227-233.
4. D. B. J. Schouten, *Exacte economie*. Pg. 148-158 and graph X.

and an exchange relation which leads to an equal division are assumed, whereas in particular the degree of specialization and the optimum exchange ratio must be explained. The problem which must still be solved is then accepted as understood in the discussed theory. Naturally, this is methodologically inadequate. It is therefore recommended when answering the fundamental questions of the comparative costs theory, not to follow the suggestions indicated in figure 11.

More interest was shown in the second answer to the three questions as complete specialization and 'fair division'. A concave path of the transformation curve is assumed. It is generally known that Haberler started this. Caves points out that three different motives may support this concave path.[5] Haberler based his theory on the effect of the law of non-proportional returns. Samuelson on differentiated factor ratios in different production sectors and levels, whereas Eckhaus and Leontier assume constant, differentiated factor ratios. We limit ourselves to Haberler and Samuelson, as their approaches provide adequate possibilities for our assessment.

Haberler's argument for the spherical path of the transformation line is simplified. The theory regarding this as expressed in 'The Theory of International Trade' means that the different final products are produced with two production means, of which only one can be re-allocated. Based on the final products *A* and *B*, the following argument applied to the concave path of the transformation line: 'The only factor of production, which is common to both *A* and *B* is labour, and – at any rate in the short run – the mobility of labour between the two branches is quite small'.[6] One can imagine this situation in such a way that *A* and *B* are produced with the aid of labour and capital. Both factors of production are given quantitatively per sector in the initial situation; capital cannot be re-allocated, but labour can. Naturally, when transferring labour the law of non-proportional returns will occur, causing the transformation line to proceed from a specific point – for example point A, in figure 11 – both bent to the left as well as to the right.

However, it is untenable to draw a concave line from axis to axis based on the produced assumptions, because – as soon as an axis is reached – the production of one final product is completely finished. However, at that moment a part of the capital goods stock – namely, that part which is present in the sector in which the production has been stopped – is no longer productively employed. This possible disequilibrium may prevent the solution of the fundamental problems of the comparative cost theory in a satisfactory way.

5. Richard E. Caves, *Trade and economic structure*, Pg. 30-37.
6. G. von Haberler, *The Theory of International Trade*. Pg. 178-179.

Caves informs us that Samuelson expressed his thoughts on the inflected transformation line in a study published in 1949.[7] This is correct, even though Samuelson together with Stolper had already earlier designed such a curve, based on the differentiated factor ratios by sector and varying according to the size of production.[8] The theory of Stolper and Samuelson is now illustrated with the aid of an example, which is designed in such a way that it also covers the opinions of Haberler regarding the effect of the law on the non-proportional returns. This has been done in table 9, which contains data for the construction of the concave transformation curves. These are shown in figure 12. The labour/capital ratio in the various countries differs according to the Heckscher/Ohlin principle. Furthermore, when a change in production is made from a certain point on the transformation curves, the law of the non-proportional returns will occur. This is apparent when one considers that originally labour and capital are exclusively applied in the c_1 sector, after which there is a gradual displacement to the c_2 sector. Then α_{c1} in both countries drops, whereas the capital coefficients in the c_1 sector remain constant. Simultaneously, α_{c2} remains unchanged and the capital coefficients in the c_2-sector increase. These changes express the effect

Table 9. Differentiated factor ratios and non-proportional returns.

Allocation of labour $\alpha c_1 . c_1 + \varkappa c_2 . c_2 = L$	Allocation of capital $\varkappa c_1 . c_1 + \varkappa c_2 . c_2 = K$	Labour for c_1	Labour for c_2	Capital for c_1	Capital for c_2
Country I	Country I	Country I			
$\frac{1}{2} . 60 + - . - = 30$	$\frac{1}{4} . 60 + - . - = 15$	30	–	15	–
$\frac{5}{18} . 45 + 1 . 17\frac{1}{2} = 30$	$\frac{1}{4} . 45 + \frac{3}{14} . 17\frac{1}{2} = 15$	$12\frac{1}{2}$	$17\frac{1}{2}$	$11\frac{1}{4}$	$3\frac{3}{4}$
$\frac{1}{6} . 30 + 1 . 25 = 30$	$\frac{1}{4} . 30 + \frac{7}{10} . 25 = 15$	5	25	$7\frac{1}{2}$	$7\frac{1}{2}$
$\frac{2}{15} . 15 + 1 . 28 = 30$	$\frac{1}{4} . 15 + \frac{45}{112} . 28 = 15$	2	28	$3\frac{3}{4}$	$11\frac{1}{4}$
$- . - + 1 . 30 = 30$	$- . - + \frac{1}{2} . 30 = 15$	–	30	–	15
Country II	Country II	Country II			
$\frac{1}{2} . 40 + - . - = 20$	$1 . 40 + - . - = 40$	20	–	40	–
$\frac{11}{30} . 30 + \frac{1}{4} . 36 = 20$	$1 . 30 + \frac{5}{18} . 36 = 40$	11	9	30	10
$\frac{11}{40} . 20 + \frac{1}{4} . 58 = 20$	$1 . 20 + \frac{10}{29} . 58 = 40$	$5\frac{1}{2}$	$14\frac{1}{2}$	20	20
$\frac{1}{5} . 10 + \frac{1}{4} . 72 = 20$	$1 . 10 + \frac{5}{12} . 72 = 40$	2	18	10	30
$- . - + \frac{1}{4} . 80 = 20$	$- . - + \frac{1}{2} . 80 = 40$	–	20	–	40

7. Paul A. Samuelson, *International Factor-Price Equalisation Once Aagain.*
8. W. Stolper and P. A. Samuelson, *Protection and Real Wages.*

of the law of non-proportional returns. Additionally, in each country and in each sector the capital/labour ratio changes with each change in production. The ideas of Haberler, Stolper and Samuelson have been included in table 9 and figure 12 respectively through the simultaneous occurrence of the law of the non-proportional returns and changes in the factor relations per sector. The examination can be continued based on the concave transformation curves.

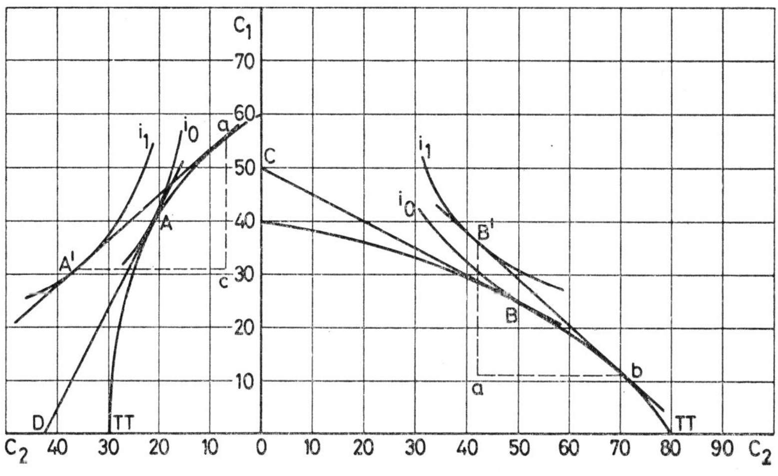

Fig. 12. Specialization of production and international trade; Heckscher/Ohlin-principle.

In order to establish the autarchic equilibrium attention is drawn to the point where the transformation line touches the highest attainable indifference curve. Assuming the already known hyperbolic indifference curve, this equilibrium is reached at points *A* (country I) and *B* (country II). Lines *AD* and *BC*, which can be continued from axis to axis – this has not been done for reasons of clarity – provide the relationship of the final products according to the transformation and indifference curves where these touch each other. Consequently, *A* and *B* form the autarchic equilibria from which the solution of the fundamental problems of the comparative cost theory must start. Given the conditions shown in figure 12, country I has a comparative cost advantage with regard to c_1 and country II regarding c_2. After all, these products are relatively cheap in the different countries. After opening the frontiers, the countries will specialize their production in the indicated direction and simultaneously, based on a certain exchange ratio, proceed to international trade. Subsequently, and using the work by Wells as an example in this connection[9], – it is usual for the domestic and international equilibrium to accept as a criterion that the marginal final product relationships are equal to the external exchange relationships. An argument in favour, is that in that situation the highest attainable indifference curve is reached in both countries by the line representing the possible final product ratio. Figure 12 meets this criterion. Country I specializes in the production of *A* towards *a*, exports a quantity c_1 amounting to *ac* and imports c_2 to a size of cA^I. Consequently, the external exchange ratio as seen from this country, is shown by aA^I. This line reaches in A^1 the highest attainable indifference curve. For country II a production specialization from *B* to *b* applies; the c_2-export amounts to *bd* and the import of c_1 reaches a size of dB^1. Consequently, and as seen from country II, an external exchange ratio is formed which is shown in line bB^1. This touches B^1 in the highest attainable indifference curve.

All this is instructive but inadequate. The above is only an approximate description of the international equilibrium situation. The problem as to why precisely on the basis of the discussed external exchange ratio with the relating production-specialization and international trade that equilibrium became possible, has so far been solved in too simple a fashion. A more penetrating examination follows in the next para.

2. The nature of equilibrium

The tools for a description of the international equilibrium consist of the transformation, the indifference, the reciprocal demand and the external exchange ratio curves. These are readily available. The introduction of the production and the consumption sectors was based on the transformation and indifference curve; the 'reciprocal demand' and the external exchange ratio line need only be added.

An attempt has already been made to describe within the scope of the Heckscher/Ohlin principle international equilibrium based on the said curves. The foundation of this was laid in a work by Meade.[10] The basis of the theory is the 'trade indifference curve'. The first impression is that this provides an extension of the tools, as a new and so far unknown, curve is added to the four. However, in fact there is no addition at all. It will become apparent that the trade indifference curve ('t.i.c.') is simply a recapitulation of the '*rd*'

9. Sidney J. Wells, *International Economics*. Pg. 41-43.
10. James Edward Meade, *A Geometry of International Trade*. Pg. 9-43 and the figures I-XVIII.

and the external exchange ratio line, without real meaning to the theory of international trade. For a description of this figure 12 provides a 't.i.c.' example in connection with figure 13. For reasons of simplicity, country II is ignored for a moment. Assuming that country I has a comparative cost advantage with regard to c_1, this country will specialize in that direction. This is shown in figure 13 in accordance with the theory which forms the

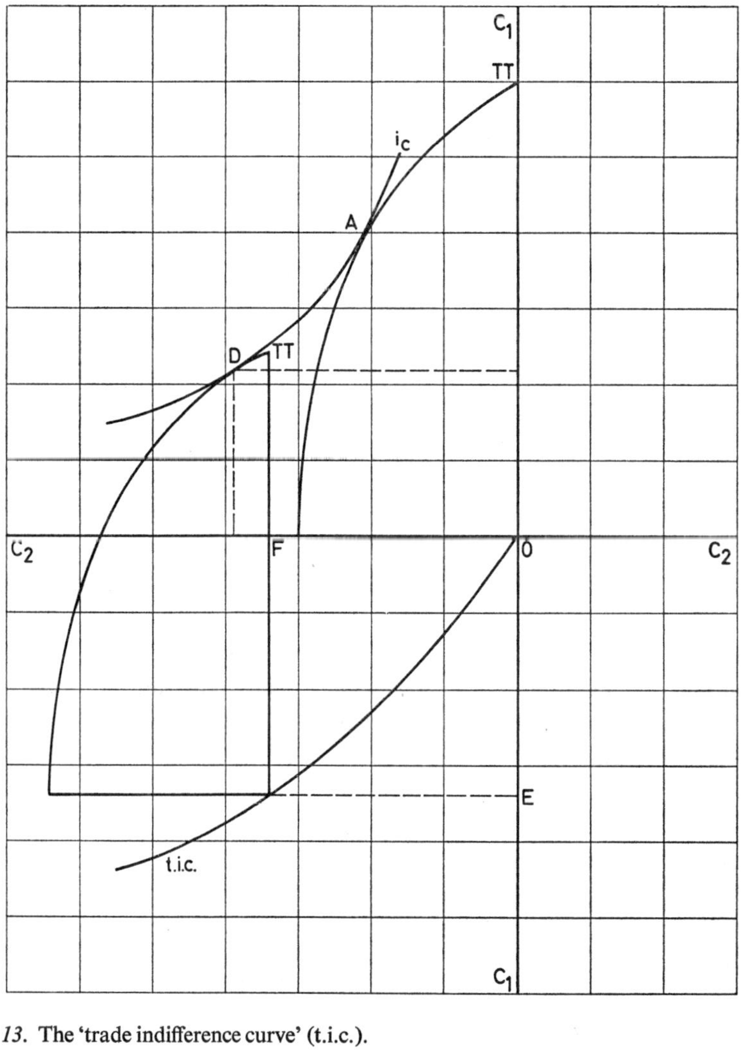

Fig. 13. The 'trade indifference curve' (t.i.c.).

basis of the 'trade indifference curve' by a displacement of the transformation line along the indifference curve – in so far as it concerns the production points – from *A* to *D*.

This displacement takes place in such a way, that the *y*-axis remains always strictly vertical and the *x*-axis precisely horizontal. The next link in the theory is that the prosperity position of the country concerned, remains constant when in point *D* – after the production specialization which has then been reached already – a quantity of c_1 amounting to *OE* is exported whilst an amount *OF* in c_2 is imported. This shows that the 't.i.c.' indicates what international trade at which degree of production specialization is required in order not to deviate from the original prosperity level. This object is achieved because the new combination of c_1 and c_2, which is available for consumption, forms a point on one and the same indifference curve as compared to the initial position. In fact the 't.i.c.', given a certain degree of production specialization, represents that amount of international trade which is considered necessary for the maintenance of prosperity by the consumption sector. From this point of view the 't.i.c.' is a 'reciprocal demand curve'. However, the 't.i.c.' also contains an indication of international trade, as this actually occurs for the maintenance of the propserity level. In this way it is an external exchange relation line. Consequently, as was stated earlier, the 't.i.c.' forms a combined reproduction of the 'reciprocal demand' and the international exchange. This peculiar combination included in the 't.i.c.' has not always been recognized in the literature, as is evident from the work by Heller.[11] We shall not pursue this matter further. It is sufficient to conclude that the 't.i.c.' is practically meaningless for the comparative cost theory and as such for the theory of international trade. It represents nothing but a coinciding '*rd*' and external ratio relation line; such a curve is of limited importance. Chapter II indicated already that for a description of the international equilibrium in particular, the different path of the '*rd*' and the external exchange ratio line – and furthermore their point of intersection – are important. The only importance of the 't.i.c.' as shown in figure 13 is that within the comparative cost theory it indicates a little more clearly than the line sections *ac* and *ae* in figure 3, the boundary between absolute and relative exploitation. This will be further explained by figure 15 but we shall first concentrate on figure 14.

The graph concerned provides, based on the transformation, the indifference, the reciprocal demand and the external exchange line, a description

11. H. Robert Heller, *International Trade; Theory and Empirical Evidence*. Pg. 61-67.

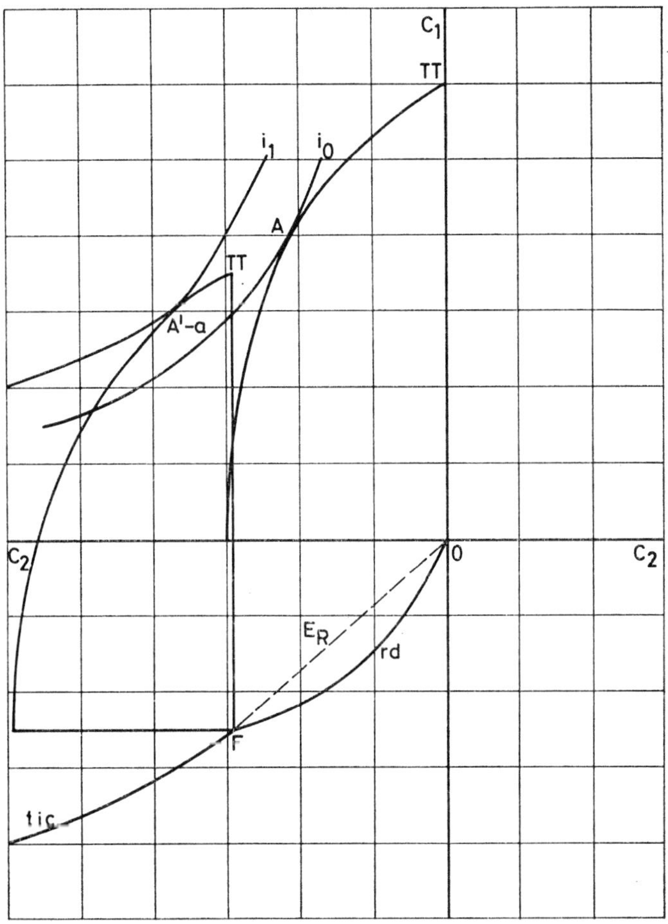

Fig. 14. Specialization of production and international trade with re-allocatable factors of production.

of the development from A to A^1, or from the autarchic to the international equilibrium as seen from country I. The production specialization from A to a and the amendment of the consumption from A to A^1 imply an international trade shown by *DF*. The size of the imports and exports is naturally precisely equal to the one shown in figure 12. As compared to the autarchic equilibrium, this all leads to a higher level of consumer demand as an indifference curve further removed from the origin is reached. In the graphical sketch the '*rd*' line is once again – as in chapter III – a cost curve indicating how much c_1 the country concerned is prepared to relinquish in order to obtain the corresponding quantity c_2. As compared to this, the E_R-curve provides a proceeds line indicating how much c_2 the country concerned actually receives for the c_1 export. As long as in figure 14 which has been developed entirely in accordance with the theory described in chapter III, the E_R-line is above the '*rd*' curve, the proceeds will outweigh the costs. As soon as the curves intersect – which is the case in point F – costs and proceeds are equal. Then, as a result of production specialization and international trade, the equilibrium A^1 is also reached.

Assuming various indifference curves, and based on a differentially displaced transformation line, it is obvious that various combinations of '*rd*' and external exchange curves are possible. This is the case with relation to the two countries which have been included in the examination. However, only those combinations in which the E_R-lines of the different lines coincide are of importance to a theory of international trade which aims at – as described in para 2 of chapter II – establishing to what extent the participating countries can improve their mutual prosperity level thanks to one another. Such a situation only presents the possibility of a simultaneous equilibrium as it enables international trade which will definitely lead to reciprocal advantage, without an economic force being exercised by the one country with regard to the other, resulting in exploitation. Figure 14 shows the relating combination of '*rd*' and E_R-curves for country I with line sections OF. Beyond point F is a 'trade indifference curve', which corresponds with the i_1-line from A^1 down. In fact, this only means that from point F the '*rd*' and the E_R-line form together an 't.i.c.'. Once again, this is theoretically unimportant as the equilibrium is already reached in F. There the question regarding the external exchange ratio, the degree of production specialization and the size of the international trade have already been answered and the analysis is completed.

So far the examination was limited to country I. As an extension of the theory, figure 15 shows the trade indifference curves of countries I and II, which correspond with those indifference lines, at which, according to figure 12, autarchic equilibrium was formed. The two inflected lines concerned include the shaded area $0G$. Further to figure 3, it may be observed that in the event of international trade based on an exchange ratio outside the shaded area DG, one country is absolutely exploited, as then the original prosperity level cannot be maintained. Only within the region DG is an increasingly prosperous international trade possible for the two countries. This means that the 't.i.c.' which correspond with the autarchic equilibrium in-

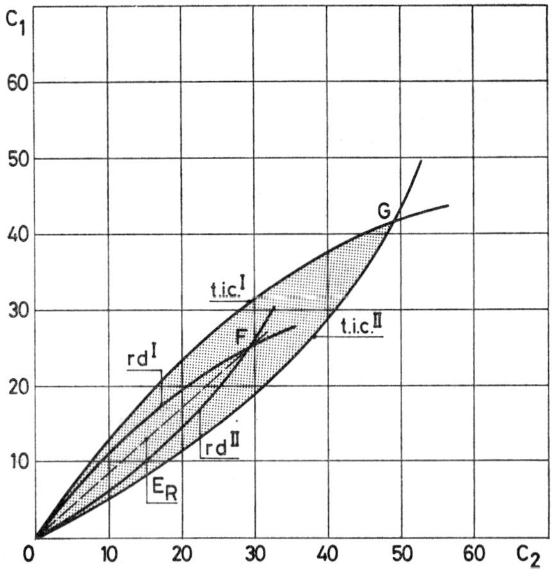

Fig. 15. Reciprocal demand and external exchange ratio based on the Heckscher/Ohlin-principle.

difference curves, form the concrete boundary between absolute and relative exploitation. Additionally, within the shaded area $0G$, is the E_R-curve, the line based on which both countries can improve their prosperity level without conflict with one another. In figure 15 the E_R-curves of the two countries coincide on the line-section $0F$, whereas the corresponding '*rd*' curves intersect in F. The effect is that simultaneously in the different countries an equality of costs in accordance with the '*rd*' and the proceeds in accordance with the E_R-curves, is achieved.

This explains the optimum external exchange ratio, the degree of production specialization and the size of the international trade more extensively than the previous para. The question remains whether the model can be criticized. The answer to this is whether the criterion above – considering the possible triple difference in the nature of the production factors – the specific of the external exchange relation, the degree of production specialization and the size of the international trade was clearly expressed.

This criterion demands in practice that in the solution of fundamental problems of the comparative cost theory, two conditions must be met in the event of original, at least given and re-allocatable production factors. In the first place there must be no mixing with non-re-allocatable production means, or international trade respectively, by substitution of the final products. In the event of different forms of international trade having various effects, this is necessary in order to be able to place them methodologically accurately in the intended model. Secondly, it is always desirable to be aware of the limitations of the entire theory with regard to the special situation of given, reallocatable production factors and this in such a way that the methodological possibility remains open of extending the theory to the third situation, in which capital is considered as being a problem. For the assessment of the theory described it is necessary to investigate to what extent these two conditions have been met in the above.

The first requirement has apparently not been met. Already at the end of chapter II it became apparent that the utilisation of advantages available in the existence of comparative cost differences, will be apparent from the net increase of final products. This was not quite the case in the above. In country I the increase of c_2 coincided with a decrease of c_1. And in country II the growth of c_1 went together with a reduction of c_1. In this manner international trade by substitution of final products and that based on the existence of comparative cost differences came within the scope of the Heckscher/Ohlin principle. Such a mixed presentation is usual in the literature as is apparent from the work by Freeman.[12] However, methodologically this mix is undesirable, as the explanation of the external exchange ratio, the international trade and the production specialization has a differing effect in different situations. This will be further apparent from the first para of the next chapter.

The second condition meant that it should always be possible to extend the theory to the situation in which one production factor is original and the other – more precisely the capital – has been derived. This is important in order to give the comparative cost theory the highest possible reality value and to combine it as far as possible with the theory of economic growth and the theory of income formation. In fact, this condition has not been met either. The comparative cost theory based on the Heckscher/Ohlin principle has been seen mostly as a key-stone and attempts have been made to extend it in two directions. A group of authors including Johnson[13], Södersten[14] and Meier[15] grafted onto the concave transformation curve a growth

12. A. Myrick Freeman, *International Trade: an Introduction to Method and Theory*. Pg.96.
13. Harry G. Johnson, *Money, trade and economic growth*. Part IV, pg. 75 etc.
14. Bo Södersten, *A study of Economic Growth and International Trade*. Pg. 30 etc. as well as *International economics*. Pg. 152-182.
15. Gerard W. Meier, *International Trade and Development*. Pg. 12 etc.

theory in an international connection. Others such as Samuelson, Meade and Hicks highlighted the development of the factor price relations. These two branches will now be briefly discussed from the point of view of the extent to which they enable a favourable link between the comparative cost theory on the one hand and the theory of economic growth and the theory of income distribution on the other.

3. Growth and income distribution

A concavely shifting transformation line is characteristic of the ideas of Johnson and Meier in particular. Something similar to this has already been demonstrated in this chapter, and figure 16 shows an example. Sometimes Södersten draws the curve concerned rectangularly decreasing from the left to the right; that is now of secondary importance.

The movement indicates economic growth. The expectation that in this manner a sensible link between the comparative cost theory and the growth

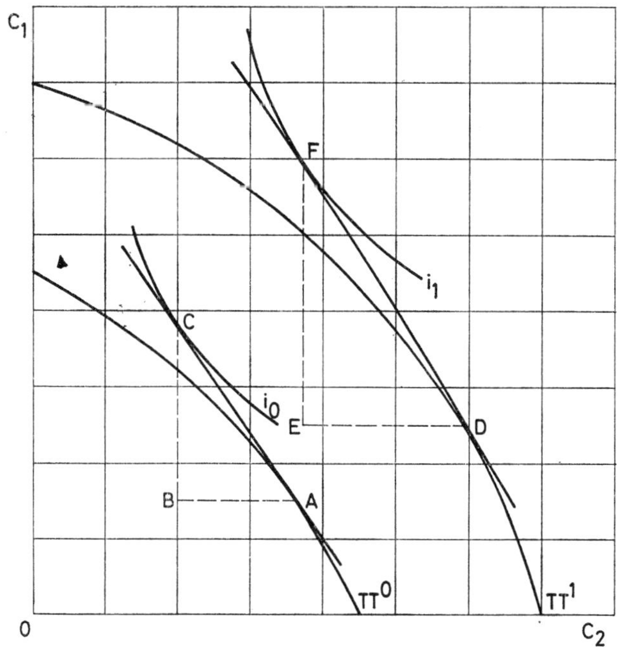

Fig. 16. Theory of comparative costs (Heckscher/Ohlin-principle) and economic growth.

theory is possible cannot be rated very highly. Already at this stage two reasons for this may be mentioned. In the first place economic growth cannot be integrated satisfactorily in the theory of international trade when capital is assumed to be given. As for the production sector, that theory simply cannot go any further than a shifting transformation curve. However, both the qualitative as well as the quantitative growth of capital then assist science as 'manna from heaven'. This is methodologically unsatisfactory, as the forming of the capital goods stock is an economic scientific problem. In addition to the shifted transformation curve the reaction of the consumption sector can then be analysed.

This leads to a second objection. Especially from the study by Johnson which was just mentioned, it is apparent that these reactions can be very varied. This implies a multitude of possibilities for the new level of production specialization, the alterations in the size of the international trade and the changes in the external exchange relation. In principle, this means an endless quibbling which is of little interest.

Van de Gevel provides the opportunity of giving these considerations deeper study.[16] The Heckscher/Ohlin principle, the argument goes, is static and as such does not provide a satisfactory basis of the analysis of a growth process over a period of time. The 'product cycle theory' comes to the rescue. A product passes through three stages. In the innovation stage it is invented and marketed as new; countries with a highly developed technical know-how then have a comparative advantage. During the growing phase production is standardized and finally the product reaches the stage of maturity. It is then suitable for mass production, owing to which developing countries could be placed in a comparatively advantageous position. Van de Gevel concludes that this theory 'has the greatest claim to a dynamic characterization' of the Heckscher/Ohlin theory.

The question remains whether this conclusion will prove to be satisfactory. This is most probably not the case from a methodological point of view, as the manner in which the time element was placed in the scientific approach was inadequate. The difference between critical and theoretical thinking is decisive in this discussion. Within the scope of critical thinking time is an historic period within which the prevailing social economic system was shaped and which is now assessed reflectively with regard to the required future development. We can determine neither the beginning nor the end ourselves; historical time is given because for us it is embodied in the event.

16. A. J. W. van de Gevel, *Internationale handel en economische groei.* Pg. 323-393.

The critical-reflective assessment can subsequently be theoretically deepened by distilling from the social/economic reality a logical description showing potential causes and effects. The implicit cause and effect can subsequently be hypothetically analyzed; the beginning and the end of it being the theoretical time which is included in the data determination and as such subject to human decision. Here the event obtains meaning in time.

The relationship between historical and theoretical time depends on the intention of bringing the results of the theoretical analysis into practice. Two opposing situations can be distinguished. It is possible that – on the one hand – the desire to acquire insight without the intention of relating theoretical knowledge to the historical situation dominates. Then the emphasis is on critical thinking; the theory can probably be limited to a statistical analysis. On the other hand it may be the express intention to apply these theories in practice. Then there is little or no room for critical thinking.

In the theory of international trade the main emphasis is on the first approach. The comparative cost theory based on the Heckscher/Ohlin principle falls short as the data determination takes place precisely on the boundary of criticism and theory. Critical thinking is inadequately developed, as – more particularly – there is no description of capital formation. The theory is inadequately placed in the historic time. Van de Gevel holds another opinion; he regrets the static nature of the analysis and subsequently the place determination in the theoretical time. The short-coming is 'the classical statistical interpretation of the concept comparative advantage, when only a timeless cross-section analysis is given of the comparative costs and a variety of dynamic elements is not taken into account'. However, the above is the real methodological shortcoming, it shows that the comparative cost theory, based on the Heckscher/Ohlin principle, remained entangled in the neoclassical method. This is even more evident in the extension in the direction of income formation.

This second branch of the discussed comparative cost theory is known as the 'factor price equalisation'. The discussion of this can take place from the autarchic equilibrium of country I according to point *A* in figure 12. The line *0A* in the graph, continued from axis to axis, can be interpreted in two ways. According to (3) it is the marginal utility ratio of the final products; if it represents the ratio of the consumption goods according to (4), it is the budget line.

$$\frac{c_2}{c_1} = \mu \tag{3}$$

$$\frac{\lambda}{1-\lambda} \cdot \frac{c_2}{c_1} = \frac{P_{c1}}{P_{c2}} \tag{4}$$

in which:

λ = fraction smaller than one, representing the part of the expendable income y, which is used for the purchase of c_2;[17]

P = the price of a final product and namely of c_1, resp. of c_2.

The equilibrium in the consumption sector is achieved when the point of intersection of the lines of the final product ratios according to (3) and (4) touches the highest attainable indifference curve. From a micro economic point of view this equilibrium is achieved because (5) has been met.

$$(5) \quad \frac{c_2}{c_1} = \qquad = \frac{P_{c1}}{P_{c2}}$$

This equation includes the known equilibrium condition that the marginal utility ratio becomes equal to the reverse of the price ratio, so that the marginal utility levelling of the last unit of money spent is reached at c_1 and c_2 respectively. There is a macro economic equilibrium because the budget line of the national spending reaches the highest attainable indifference curve. As a result of this the sectorial price sums $C_1 \cdot p_{c1}$, $C_2 \cdot p_{c2}$ respectively, or those parts of the national income which flow to the different production sectors, have been determined.

Figure 12 has been based on the already discussed hyperbolic indifference curve; in fact this means a simplified presentation of the above. Generally speaking, it has been assumed that the curves indicating the final product ratios according to (3) and (4), have indeed a point of intersection, by a different path. A special case of this is that these curves coincide. In figure 12 this situation occurs as a consequence of the chosen indifference curve. On the one hand this is the result of the circumstance that the location of the indifference curves with regard to one another depends on the absolute value of the product of the co-ordinates; naturally a curve will be higher when the product is larger. Additionally, the chosen hyperbolic indifference curve is characterized by a constant product of co-ordinates. Furthermore, the product of co-ordinates can be calculated at each point of the budget line. As this curve slopes downwards from left to right, that product is maximized precisely in the centre. It is there that the highest attainable hyperbolic indifference curve is touched. All this means that half of the expendable income will be used for the purchase of c_1 or c_2 respectively, so that $\lambda = \frac{1}{2}$. As a result the lines indicating the ratios of the final product according to (3) and (4) coincide.

17. If $\lambda y = c_1 \cdot p_{c1}$ then $(1-\lambda)y = c_2 \cdot p_{c2}$ applies. From which (4) can be concluded.

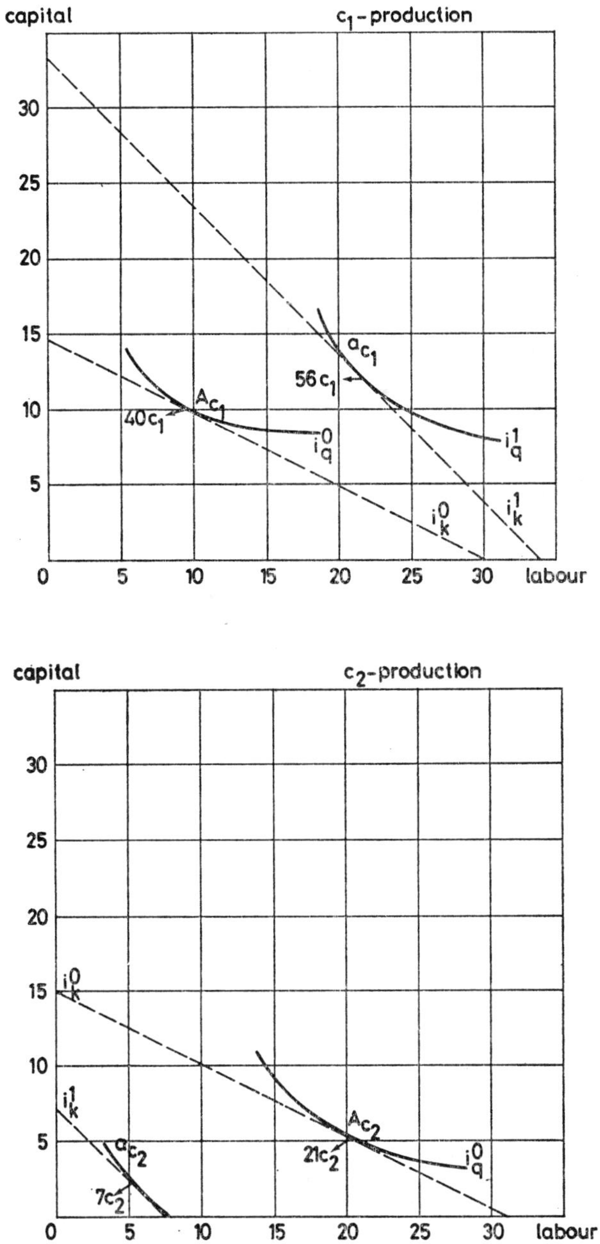

Fig. 17. Isoquant and income formation.

In addition it is important to show how within the different sectors the rewards received are distributed between labour and capital. When considering this problem the isoquant must be included in the consideration. The isoquant has been defined as a curve representing two production factors in ever varying combinations when the quantity of final product to be produced remains constant. Figure 17 shows based on table 9 and figure 12 the isoquants for both the autarchic and the international equilibrium with relation to country I.

The lines concerned are convex as compared to the origin. This type of representation is normal in the literature and we will not expand on it.

Table 9 implies that in the autarchic situation labour is incorporated at point A_{c1} 9 labour and 10 capital; point A_{c2} shows the allocation of 21 labour and 5 capital. The question remains why this factor ratio has been chosen. The answer to this is limited by the assumption that the means of production are assumed to be homogeneous; consequently the various sectors will receive an equal remuneration. The iso cost curve is of importance to the graphical description. This shows great similarity with the budget line, as it includes an indication of the production means which can be attained with a specific amount to be spent and at given factor remunerations. In figure 17 they have been drawn as i_k-lines. The theory is now analogous to the considerations regarding the consumption equilibrium. Since the search was there for a connection between the budget line with an indifference curve, it now concerns a point of intersection of an iso cost curve with an isoquant, in order to reach the highest possible production level. The equal remuneration of labour and capital in the c_1 and c_2 sector respectively, means that the iso cost lines of the sectors are parallel. After all, these lines indicate the cost ratios and these are the same in both sectors. However, many iso cost lines may meet this condition, consequently, the curve corresponding with the optimum allocation of labour and capital is therefore still unknown.

The sectorial income distribution, provided above, implies a specific production with relating isoquants. In figure 17 these are the curves i_k^0 for the production of 40_{c1} or 21_{c2} respectively. Based on the given sectorial incomes and at different factor quantities and corresponding remuneration standards (these are the remunerations per unit of production factor), it is possible to draw various iso costs lines, touching the isoquants concerned. As the path of these curves is smoother, as is the case in figure 17, the remuneration degree of capital will increase and that of labour decrease. This implies that capital is gradually being replaced by labour. The changes in price and quantity determine together the optimum combination of the production factors. For a description of this it can be assumed that each time a unit of capital is replaced by labour, which is required compensatingly in order to maintain the production. The convex path of the isoquant means that this quantity of compensating labour increases continuously. Additionally, the remaining capital will be used based on a progressively increasing remuneration rate. The replacement of capital by labour with this background reaches an optimum point, when the changes in the price amounts – the units of capital or labour respectively multiplied by their remuneration standards – are equal.

It is obvious that this concerns an optimum point, because, as long as the indicated equilibrium has not been reached, the replacement of the one production factor by the other is advantageous. As soon as equilibrium has been reached, each factor is rewarded in accordance with the marginal product, so that the above theory includes an application of the marginal productivity theory. The income forming in the autarchic situation in this manner is shown in figure 17 by the iso costs lines $i_k{}^0$.

Subsequently the frontiers are opened; then production specialization and international trade follow with the result that a_{c1} and a_{c2} respectively in figure 17 represent the new equilibrium income distribution. It is now desirable to include the situation within country II in the examination, which is possible by the introduction of the Edgeworth/Bowley-diagram. This has been done in figure 18, which has been arranged in such a way that the isoquants and the iso costs curves relating to c_1 and c_2 have been included for each country. Such a representation is normal in the theory of international trade. Additionally figure 18 includes these graphical representations – in direct connection to table 9 and figure 12 for countries I and II. The inflexed dotted lines of $c^0 1$ to $c^0 2$ indicate the allocation of the production factors; the combinations x are shown in table 9. Once again points A and B refer to the autarchic equilibrium; there the different isoquants intersect each other. Additionally, the iso costs lines pass through these points, which coincide as a result of the equal remuneration of the homogeneous production factors. Initially, the remuneration of capital is relatively high in country I, which is expressed in the rather flat path of the $i_k{}^0$-line. In country II the autarchic income conditions are just the reverse. Additionally production specialization and international trade – as described above, more particularly as an explanation of figure 12 – cause a relative improvement of the labour reward in country I; in country II the same is the case with capital remuneration. The result of all this is approximately equal income ratios, which have been

Fig. 18a. Country I.

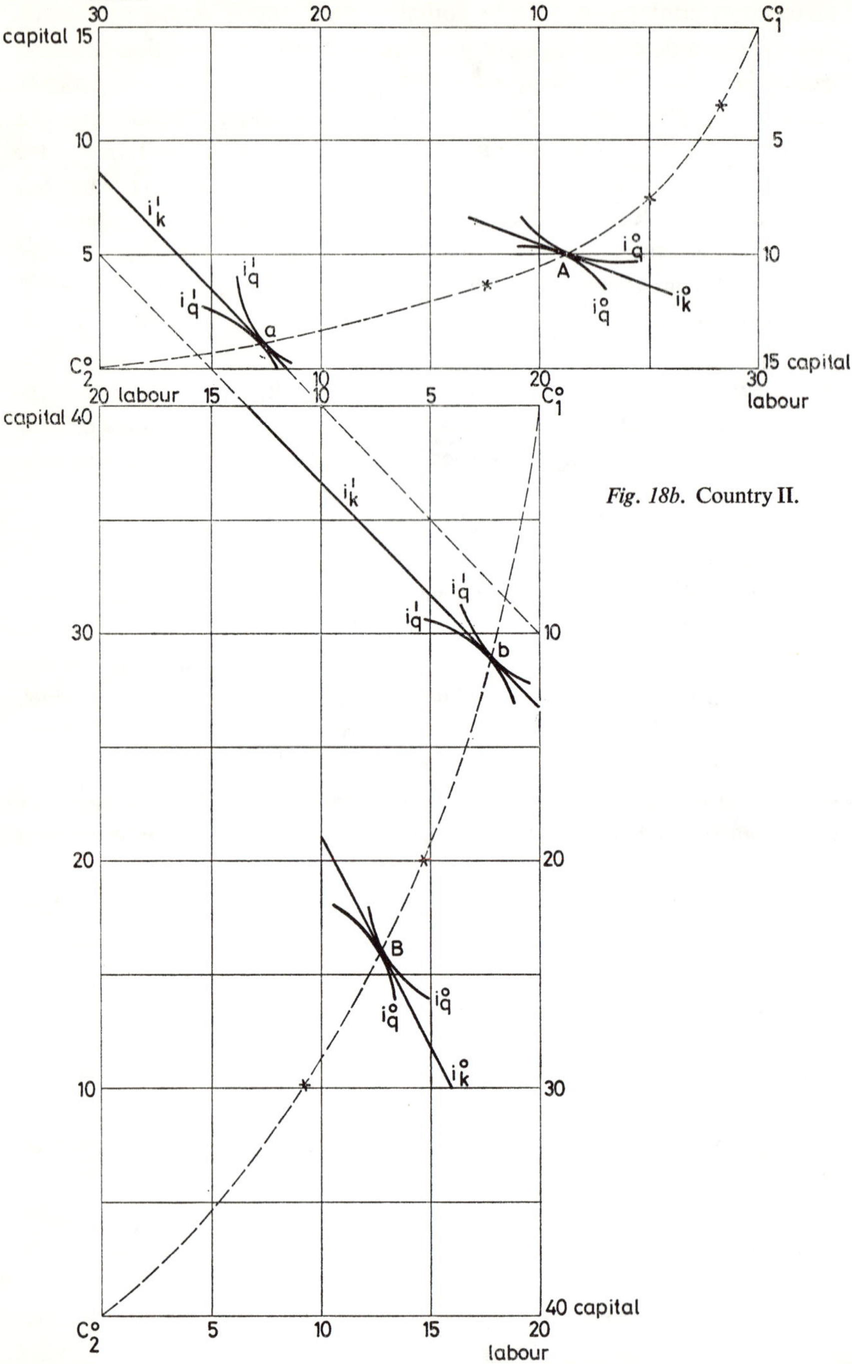

Fig. 18b. Country II.

Fig. 18a/18b. Edgeworth/Bowley-diagram.

indicated by the parallel i_k^1-curves. This is known as the 'factor price equalisation'. The general effect of the international trade theory based on the Heckscher/Ohlin principle becomes evident. The initial point is the uneven factor ratios for the individual countries. When the labour/capital ratio is large, the commodities which are labour intensive to produce are cheap and the relative labour reward low. When this country decides on production specialization and international trade with countries with different factor ratios, the labour-intensively produced commodities can be profitably sold there. The prices of these products will increase, as well as the relative reward of labour. Owing to that the price and income ratios consequently tend to uniformity in the individual countries.

An assessment of the above can be made from the nature of the data selection. Following the lead of Eucken in this connection, there a triple difference is possible.[18] In the first place the intentions of the economic subjects are important, or – in concreto – optimum consumer demand and income formation. The first objective can be achieved by a complete application of the expendable income and – as such – marginal utility equalisation. The second objective is achieved by full employment and equal marginal costs or marginal productivities. A second collection of data concerns the quantitative and qualitative availability of production factors. In this connection labour and capital within the scope of the Heckscher/Ohlin principle were considered as given from both points of view. The third data group concerns the social economic order, which presupposed implicitly in the way described above that an allocation of the factors of production was possible in order to realize the described intentions of consumers and producers.

It belongs to the nature of this choice of data – with reference to the introduction to this study and the discussion of the economic growth in accordance with the displacing transformation curve in this para – that it takes place on the boundary line of theory and criticism. That is why it implies that the data are directly independent data, with exclusively strictly logical properties and relations. Such a formulation is entirely in accordance with the neoclassical method; the two branches of the discussed comparative cost theory point in the same direction. Consequently, the theory of international trade based on the Heckscher/Ohlin principle has four fundamental characteristics from a scientific philosophical point of view:

- it presupposes the economic process as a strictly logically organized whole, in which a mathematically based analysis can provide all information.

18. Walter Eucken, *Die Grundlagen der Nationalökonomie*. Pg. 128-134.

Within the scope of international trade theory the work of Pearce is a living example of this.[19] According to this opinion only a purely-rational criticism is possible within the economic science;

- it requires 'freedom of value' in the sense that the analysis will not be influenced by the social philosophy held by the scientist;
- the equilibrium in the production and consumption sector is entirely reached within a micro-economic framework, so that there is only room for a descriptive macro economy. That, in fact, was so in the above case;
- hypothetically, the economic process is entirely outside history; historical progress has no real influence. This is especially apparent in the discussion of economic growth owing to the lack of space for critical thinking.

Remaining within the theory of international trade, it now becomes essential to widen the horizon by introducing capital formation as a problem. This will call for another description of production specialization, international trade, economic growth and income distribution than the one given above, as well as a methodological re-orientation of the above four points.

19. S. F. Pearce, *International Trade.*

VI. INTERNATIONAL EQUILIBRIUM AT COMPARATIVE COST DIFFERENCES

As seen in the introduction to the previous chapter the production factors are:

- non re-allocatable, so that they can only be used for the production of c_1 or c_2;
- or original, at least quantitatively given and re-allocatable;
- or re-allocatable, when – assuming two production factors – the one is original and the other one derived.

As was said earlier, this differentiation runs like a thread through our study. The first possibility was discussed in chapters III and IV. The result of international trade was the substitution of final products; the analysis of this situation is outside the comparative cost theory. The last chapter showed that so far no theoretically satisfactory solution to the fundamental problems of the comparative cost theory has been provided based on original, at least quantitatively given and re-allocatable production factors.

The study will continue from this point.

1. The optimum exchange ratio

The comparative cost theory, as developed according to the Heckscher/Ohlin principle based on the concave transformation curve, shows two remarkable shortcomings. In the first place it contains a mixture of international trade by substitution of final products and the utilisation of advantages which are present in the existence of comparative cost differences. Assuming given re-allocatable production factors, it is desirable to purify the comparative cost theory from this mixture, in order to achieve a theoretically correct description of the optimum external exchange ratio, the degree of production specialization and the size of the international trade. This paragraph is devoted to this subject. Secondly, the entire theory stopped short in the neo-classical methodologistic framework as expressed in the link between the growth theory and the theory of income formation. It is desirable to review this method of working. This is possible by the introduction of capital formation as a problem, additionally in the light of new methodological requirements which must be laid down for economic thinking. A further explanation of this is the theme for the second and third para of this chapter.

The utilisation of advantages due to the existence of comparative cost differences – as we saw already at the end of chapter II – leads to the result that production specialization and international trade cause a net increase of the commodity which was in the autarchic situation produced under relatively unfavourable circumstances. This was already apparent from the explanation of figure 4, when from the equilibrium situations *A* and *B* production specialization and international trade was decided. This took place based on an exchange ratio $c_1 : c_2$. The question was not solved as to why this ratio was optimum, in the sense that it caused international economic equilibrium, as in the final situation there was for neither of the participating countries any reason for change in production or consumption. Additionally, in chapter II labour was still the only production factor. As for this last point, the theory was already extended in the last chapter by the introduction of capital in figure 11 and the subsequent explanation. The study will continue from that point. Table 10 shows the labour and capital coefficients, as well as the available quantities of labour and capital.

Table 10. Specialization of productions and international trade with differences in comparative costs.

Period	Country I $\alpha c_1 = \frac{1}{2}$; $\alpha c_2 = 1$; $L = 30$ $\varkappa c_1 = \frac{1}{4}$; $\varkappa c_2 = \frac{1}{2}$; $K = 15$				Country II $\alpha c_1 = 1$; $\alpha c_2 = \frac{1}{2}$; $L = 40$ $\varkappa c_1 = 2$; $\varkappa c_2 = 1$; $K = 80$				Trade	
	Production		Consumption		Production		Consumption			
	c_1	c_2	c_1	c_2	c_1	c_2	c_1	c_2	c_1	c_2
0	30	15	30	15	20	40	20	40	–	–
1	36	12	30	18	17	46	23	40	6	6
2	42	9	30	21	14	52	26	40	12	12
3	48	6	30	24	11	58	29	40	18	18
4	54	3	30	27	8	64	32	40	24	24
5	60	0	30	30	5	70	35	40	30	30

Additionally, period 0 indicates which quantities of c_1 and c_2 are produced in accordance with points *A* and *B* of figure 11 in the autarchic situation.

It is the aim of this para to achieve straightforward determination of the real external exchange ratio of production specialization and international trade based on comparative cost differences within the scope of the Heckscher/Ohlin principle and according to the neo-classical method. Clarity in this context means the substitution of final products remaining entirely outside the analysis. Consequently, the theory which now follows has been based on two initial points:

- the maximization of utility is a criterion for economic equilibrium and the hyperbolic indifference curve is maintained for its analysis;
- labour and capital are both accepted as given. The size of each is stated in the heading of table 10.

The difference between this and the following paragraphs is that at a later stage the latter initial points will be changed, causing the abandonment of the rigid limits of the Heckscher/Ohlin principle and the neo-classical method. However this is not the case for the time being.

Once again, the transformation, the indifference, the reciprocal demand and the external exchange curves serve as tools for the description of international equilibria. Additionally, the description immediately follows the end of chapter II, where a description of the re-allocation of the production factors was provided. This resulted in country I restricting the c_2 production for specialization in c_1. An analogous specialisation of the production of c_2 took place in country II. Based on table 10 and figure 19 this can now be further worked out. In the figure concerned, line section Aa^i indicates to what extent country I can specialize on the production of c_1. This possibility depends on the autarchic equilibrium situation on the one hand and the intersection of the transformation line at the y-axis on the other hand. In an analogous manner line section Bb^1 indicates the specialization possibilities on c_2 for country II. This means that the transformation and indifference curves have already acquired a place in the study.

Seen from the production sector, the indicated specialization possibilities are present both from a micro as well as macro point of view. From a micro point of view, this is the case because of the differentiated technical suitability of labour and capital, or the existence of comparative cost differences in accordance with the views expressed by Ricardo. The production specialization can be determined from a macro point of view owing to the quantitatively differentiated factor relationships in accordance with the theory of Heckscher and Ohlin.

Country I may extend the c_1 production by 30 units; as is shown in figure 19a by the line section $0a$. In order to benefit from the advantages of com-

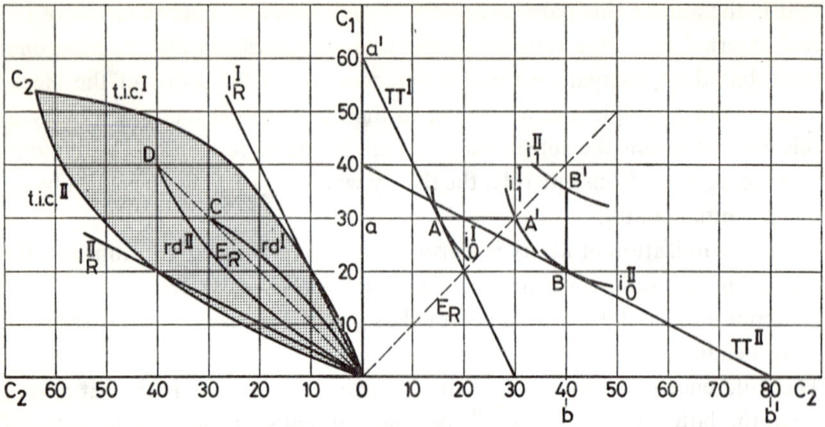

Fig. 19a/19b. The optimum exchange ratio at differences in comparative costs.

parative cost differences, this country will export the relating quantity c_1 based on an exchange ratio which enables net increase of c_2. Table 10 describes the production specialization and international trade in this way. Each time c_1 production increases by 6 units, so simultaneously c_2 production is reduced by 3 units. Country II specializes in an analogous manner on the production of c_2. This is indicated by figures in table 10; the graphical representation requires further explanation.

It must be stated, as an introduction, that the boundary between absolute and relative exploitation can be shown in two different ways. The first possibility was dealt with originally in chapter II, when in the Ricardian approach the boundary was indicated by I_R-curves and was consequently based on cost ratios. In figure 19a this has been done again, based on an objective value concept – in the sense that the value ratio of the commodities is exclusively determined by the real costs – the I_R-lines apparently form the boundary between absolute and relative exploitation. As these are different in the individual countries, an exchange ratio must be established between them, in order to enable international trade to take place with reciprocal advantage. The second possibility for a boundary determination was discussed in the previous chapter. We were then concerned with the construction of 'trade indifference curves' by a displacement of the transformation lines along the original indifference curves. The absolute and relative exploitation were separately based on the utility ratio of the commodities, which is expressed in the indifference curves concerned. This method is followed in the figures 13 and 15, the discussed trade indifference curves are also drawn in figure 19a. The various methods for boundary determination are based on totally different value assessments and are consequently independent of one another. This is fairly obvious from figure 19a, as there the I_R-lines even pass through the *0G* area. Naturally, the second method for the indication of the demaraction line between absolute and relative exploitation will be followed, in accordance with the actual theory of value.

Subsequently, the '*rd*'$^{-I}$ line in figure 19a represents the decline of the marginal utility of c_2 in country I if the production is specialized and international trade occurs in the manner indicated.

In this way, also the '*rd*'- and the E_R-curve have acquired a place in the analysis. Again the indicated decline in marginal utility is apparent where c_2 increases and c_1 remains constant. This net c_2-increase, which is the result of production specialization along part Aa^1 of the transformation curve and simultaneous international trade based on the common E_R-line, is represented by the line section AA^1. As with the description of international trade by substitution of final products, the point of intersection of the '*rd*'- and the E_R-line – i.c. point *C* – is of decisive importance. Intentionally a construction is chosen in figure 19 when the two countries do not simultaneously reach this point. This expresses the theoretical line of thought which is developed here and which also applies to countries of different size.

As a result of the above construction of the optimum exchange ratio, the degree of production specialisation and the size of the international trade is in principle a 'general theory'. In it, the country which first reaches the above point of intersection, will determine the limit of production specialization and the volume of trade. In figure 19 this is the case for country I; if it continued trading beyond point *c*, this would mean substitution of final products as the limit of the production specialization is reached in *c*. Beyond this point and in order not to end up on a lower indifference curve than the one already reached by A^1, country I will only be prepared to trade on the basis of a considerable improvement in the external exchange ratio. After all, so far this country acquired c_2 without sacrifice of c_1; however, this situation ended in *c* or in A^1 respectively. However, as will become apparent later such a continuation is not possible.

In the meantime country II has specialized production along the line section Bb^1 in the direction of c_2. International trade based on the E_R-line *DC* in figure 19a – which as in the previous chapter consists of two coinciding national external exchange relationships which correspond with the '*rd*'^{I} and the '*rd*'^{II} curve – leads in country II to a net increase of c_1.

This has been shown in figures in table 10 and graphically in figure 19b by line section BB^1. Apparently, production specialization and international trade, which continue beyond what is indicated in table 10 and figure 19, is not possible, as after point *c* – given the situation in country I – the external exchange lines no longer coincide.

The above provides a purely theoretical reply to the problems regarding the optimum exchange ratio, the degree of production specialization and the size of international trade within the framework of the comparative cost theory in the event of given, re-allocatable production factors. The essence of the line of thought can be summarized in a few conclusions. The optimum real external exchange ratio is formed by the coincidence of national external product curves. Certain national 'reciprocal-demand' cost lines correspond to this. When the E_R- and the '*rd*'-line of a specific country intersect – which is the case as soon as the production is totally specialized – then international trade can only continue by substitution of final products. This requires a considerable improvement of the exchange ratio for the country concerned, which cannot be pursued as the national E_R-lines no longer coincide. As soon as a country has reached the point of intersection of the '*rd*' and the E_R-line, it has reached the limit for production specialization and trade across the frontiers.

2. Revision of the comparative cost theory

Chapter V showed that the comparative cost theory based on original – at least quantitatively given – and re-allocatable production factors, displays two essential shortcomings in the normal presentation. In the first place, it contains a mixing of the final product substitution and international trade based on comparative cost differences. For a theoretically correct indication of the external exchange ratio the degree of production specialization and the size of the trade across the frontiers it is advisable to separate final products substitution. The last paragraph was devoted to that subject. The second shortcoming, especially when observing the development in the direction of economic growth and income distribution, indicates that the analysis got stuck in a neo-classical methodological framework. As a result of this, the third possibility regarding the nature of the production factors – when capital in particular is considered as a problem – has so far hardly found a place in the comparative cost theory. The elimination of this shortcoming forms the subject of this paragraph.

All this means a certain amount of re-assessment of the comparative cost theory from a general and a specific point of view. In the general sense, it concerns breaking away from the traditional methodological framework, which is in principle, desirable with regard to the entire economic science. The neo-classical mode of thinking, with four characteristic basic points which were mentioned at the end of the last chapter, is becoming increasingly unsuitable for a developing economic science in accordance with the requirements of the present time. The desire for methodological re-orientation forms the general framework for a re-assessment of economic thinking.

In a special way, or in practice with relation to the theory of comparative costs, renewal possibilities can be raised by the introduction of capital as problem – as a third possibility regarding the nature of production factors. This implicitly means a renewed relationship with economic growth and income distribution. We shall examine this further, and the consideration shows a close relationship with the appendix 'Critical method and macro economy' taken from our 'waardering van het economisch denken'. In both cases, in principle, the same subject is being raised, namely the description of the economic process with capital as 'vorgetane Arbeit' (labour required for the production of capital goods). The indication of this is that part of the available work is used for the production of capital goods, thus resulting in roundabout production. The crux of the matter is now to give the theory of the appendix concerned, an international dimension.

By introducing capital as 'vorgetane Arbeit' recent social economic history is revealed. Even though at first glance this seems rather remote from our subject, it is worthwhile considering some of its main lines, especially in connection with the income distribution, which will be discussed later. Western industrial development is characterized by a growing tension between labour and capital. This is because labour was withdrawn from the production of consumption goods in order to be employed in the investment sector. The manner in which this occurs always depends to a large extent on the dominating social concepts and the structure of society.

It is a historic fact of western industrial development that the initiative for the above described re-allocation of labour, has been mainly taken by entrepreneurs. This appeared to be somewhat coercive to the employees' group, especially at the beginning of industrialisation, the labour factor was characterized by a certain degree of submissiveness.

The roundabout production additionally required monetary saving by which, amongst other things, the labour, which had been employed for the production of capital goods could be rewarded. Naturally, labour itself could not provide these savings; others provided the required amount at a reasonable rate of interest. All this provided a basis for tension between entrepreneurs and providers of capital on the one hand and the labour group on the other. From the end of the eighteenth century to the present this tension has shown itself as a thread running through the history of the rise of western industrialism. The manner in which the employees group was incorporated in the development process forms the basic issue within the field of tension. The dissatisfaction expressed over the years, shows three characteristic aspects.

These are the contents, the object and the proposed changes. In fact, criticism emerged in a three-fold form:

- the labour class is threatened in its physical existence. Initially this had the main emphasis. A constructive proposal for social reform could not yet be offered. The greatest injustices were alleviated more emotionally than scientifically by Christian charity, the care of socially-conscious employers and mutual aid;
- from a Marxian point of view, private property forms the deepest cause of the tension. Capitalist society contains an antagonism between labour and capital. However, this antagonism will find its solution in a historical determined economic development causing the collapse of the existing system and the establishment of the communistic society with the collective ownership of the factors of production;
- the cause of the tension is the subjectivity of the employees to an economic power in the hands of the entrepreneurs and providers of capital, according to Dahrendorf in 'Soziale Klassen und Klassenkonflikt in der heutigen Gesellschaft'. This differs from the Marxian theory, because tension is not the result of the nature of ownership, but of the structure of economic power. Additionally a change is not historically necessary. Ideas are inclined to lead towards participation and co-control.

The labour/capital relationship as it emerged in the western economic system is a source of the above tension. Within this system the labour group must obtain its living on a labour contract basis and work with means of production which belong to others, under an authority which is predominantly not elected by the group.

In the meantime an evolution has taken place with regard to the three critical points – the income level, the system of ownership and the structure of economic power – with the result that the workers whilst retaining a certain amount of tension, are identified with to some extent the prevailing social economic system. The threat to their physical existence belongs mostly to the past, the ownership of the means of production is no longer completely capitalistic, whereas participation and sharing in the control have increased. Yet, the distribution of income, the ownership relationships and the authority structure still present many problems. Within economic science the first point is especially important. In the theory of international trade, where capital is considered as being 'vorgetane Arbeit', the possibilities for economic growth by roundabout production and – in the realisation of these – tensions in the distribution of incomes demand attention. A theoretical approximation of these can be based on an indication of the following symbols and concepts:

α = labour coefficient: in the numerator, the labour required for the production of the final product stated in the denominator. Sectorally, this coefficient is indicated by c_1, c_2 and i;

$\varkappa$ = capital coefficient: in the numerator, the capital required for the production of the final product stated in the denominator. The sector indication is as with the labour coefficient;

ε = a fraction for the indication of the part of the labour potential which works in the c_2-sector;

β = a fraction for the indication of the part of the labour potential which works in the investment sector;

ω = a fraction representing the capital consumption in the c_2-sector;

μ = the ratio in which c_2 and c_1 is demanded by the consumption sector when in equilibrium;

I = gross investments, or the production of capital goods;

D = depreciations; these include capital consumption in connection with production. Capital goods which are eligible for total depreciation because they have reached the end of their life, are indicated by D;

T = the life of capital goods. This is here always hypothetically set at three terms ($3t$);

K = capital goods supply, in so far as this is being used in the production of final products;

L = labour potential. Further to the above, this is here hypothetically always set at sixty ($60\,l$ – country I) or eighty ($80\,l$ – country II) labour units.

Subsequently, relationships between these concepts for the benefit of the theoretical analysis must be described. Methodologically this is an important moment, as now the concepts are taken from their historic context for the sake of an abstract-theoretical approach.

$$(1)\quad \alpha_{c1}\, C_1 = (1-\varepsilon-\beta)\, L$$

$$(2)\quad \alpha_{c2}\, C_2 = \varepsilon\, L$$

$$(3)\quad \alpha_i\, I \quad = \beta\, L$$

$$(4)\quad \varkappa_{c1}\, C_1 = (1-\omega)\, D$$

$$(5)\quad \varkappa_{c2}\, C_2 = \omega\, D$$

$$(6)\qquad D = \frac{1}{T} K$$

$$(7)\qquad \Delta K = \text{I previous period} - D$$

$$(8)\qquad \frac{c_2}{c_1} = \mu$$

Eight equations are important to a macro theoretical discussion of the labour/capital ratio; in which (1), (2) and (3) represent the allocation of labour. Subsequently (4) and (5) include an indication of the capital allocation. In equation (6) capital allocation has been defined as it takes place in the production of final products according to (4) and (5). In reality the capital goods supply consists of a number of produced production means which has been employed for the production of the final products. As indicated in equation (7) the calculation of the mutation in this supply within a specific period of time must be based on the gross investments in the preceding period. The totally depreciated capital goods are deducted from that. Finally (8) show in which ratio the final products are demanded by the consumers at economic equilibrium.

Based on this model, economic growth and income formation can acquire a place in the theory of international trade – and as such more particularly in the comparative cost theory – without the objections attached thereby to the Heckscher/Ohlin principle. However, many problems then arise simultaneously. Owing to this, there is a need for simplification while maintaining and emphasizing the reality of the solution of the three basic problems of the comparative cost theory. It concerns eight points:

1. an economic process in at least two countries;
2. in each country at least two final products;
3. in each country at least a two-fold production column;
4. in each country a sectorially differentiated technical progress;
5. the development of the price ratios in an autarchic connection;
6. introduction of production specialization based on comparative cost differences and relating as such to international trade;
7. the development of price ratios in an international environment;
8. income distribution with production specialization and technical development.

In a general form the model applies for the countries I and II (point I), when we maintain that country I has 60 and country II 80 labour units. In both countries final products c_1 and c_2 can be produced with labour and capital. That is indicated with the production functions (1), (2), (4) and (5). Equation (3) relates to the capital formation. After the capital goods have been supplied, the final products are produced with their employment. In this way we have a two-fold production column (point 3). All this is shown in figures in table 11. Let us assume that in period 0 labour is the only scarce production factor, in the sense that there is a lack of technical knowledge and/or spirit of enterprise for placing a part of the labour in an investment sector to be created. This situation is identical – with regard to the final product ratio – to the one of period 0 in table 10 and the points A and B in figure 19b.

A^1 and B^1 in table 11 represents the already described production specialization and international trade without roundabout production. However, this is only intended to form a link with the above. It would seem to be better to assume now that no such opening of the frontiers takes place, which is the reason why it is no longer shown in figure 21. In fact, this means an identification of the geographical areas of production and consumption in the situation concerned and is not entirely divorced from reality. In an underdeveloped society with a simple production structure, a primitive transport system and a consumer demand which is mainly directed towards fulfilling the basic necessities, the areas concerned will be more or less equal.

For developed economies this is not the case. For a description of that, we assume a technical progress within closed frontiers in the periods 1 to 5 incl.

Table 11. Specialized roundabout production and international trade.

	Country I Data						Variables								Trade
t	αc_1	αc_2	α_1	$\varkappa c_1$	$\varkappa c_2$	$\varkappa$	c_1	c_2	ε	β	ω	I	K	D	c_1
0	1	2	—	—	—	$\frac{1}{2}$	30	15	$\frac{1}{2}$	—	—	—	—	—	—
A_1	1	—	—	—	—	1	60	—	—	—	—	—	—	—	30
1	1	2	$\frac{1}{2}$	—	—	$\frac{1}{2}$	24	12	$\frac{2}{5}$	$\frac{1}{5}$	—	24	—	—	—
2			$\frac{1}{2}$	$\frac{1}{7}$	$\frac{1}{2}$	$\frac{4}{11}$	44	16	$\frac{2}{5}$	$\frac{1}{5}$	$\frac{1}{2}$	24	24	8	—
3			$\frac{1}{2}$	$\frac{1}{7}$	$\frac{1}{2}$	$\frac{5}{21}$	64	20	$\frac{2}{5}$	$\frac{1}{5}$	$\frac{1}{2}$	24	48	16	—
4			$\frac{1}{2}$	$\frac{1}{7}$	$\frac{1}{2}$	$\frac{2}{7}$	84	24	$\frac{2}{5}$	$\frac{1}{5}$	$\frac{1}{2}$	24	72	24	—
5	$\frac{2}{7}$	1	$\frac{1}{2}$	$\frac{1}{7}$	$\frac{1}{2}$	$\frac{2}{7}$	84	24	$\frac{2}{5}$	$\frac{1}{5}$	$\frac{1}{2}$	24	72	24	—
D_1	$\frac{2}{7}$	—	$\frac{1}{2}$	$\frac{1}{7}$	—	1	168	—	—	$\frac{1}{5}$	—	24	72	24	84

	Country II Data						Variables								Trade
t	αc_1	αc_2	α_1	$\varkappa c_1$	$\varkappa c_2$	$\varkappa$	c_1	c_2	ε	β	ω	I	K	D	c_1
0	2	1	—	—	—	2	20	40	$\frac{1}{2}$	—	—	—	—	—	—
B_1	2	1	—	—	—	$1\frac{1}{7}$	5	70	$\frac{7}{8}$	—	—	—	—	—	30
1	2	1	$\frac{1}{2}$	—	—	2	16	32	$\frac{2}{5}$	$\frac{1}{5}$	$\frac{1}{2}$	32	—	—	—
2			$\frac{1}{2}$	$\frac{1}{2}$	$\frac{1}{6}$	$2\frac{1}{2}$	$21\frac{1}{3}$	$53\frac{1}{3}$	$\frac{2}{5}$	$\frac{1}{5}$	$\frac{1}{2}$	32	32	$10\frac{2}{3}$	—
3			$\frac{1}{2}$	$\frac{1}{2}$	$\frac{1}{6}$	$2\frac{4}{5}$	$26\frac{1}{3}$	$74\frac{2}{3}$	$\frac{2}{5}$	$\frac{1}{5}$	$\frac{1}{2}$	32	64	$21\frac{1}{3}$	—
4			$\frac{1}{2}$	$\frac{1}{2}$	$\frac{1}{6}$	3	32	96	$\frac{2}{5}$	$\frac{1}{5}$	$\frac{1}{2}$	32	96	32	—
5	1	$\frac{1}{3}$	$\frac{1}{2}$	$\frac{1}{2}$	$\frac{1}{6}$	3	32	96	$\frac{2}{5}$	$\frac{1}{5}$	$\frac{1}{2}$	32	96	32	—
E_1	1	$\frac{1}{3}$	$\frac{1}{2}$	$\frac{1}{2}$	$\frac{1}{6}$	$1\frac{1}{11}$	4	180	$\frac{3}{4}$	$\frac{1}{5}$	$\frac{15}{16}$	32	96	32	84

of table 11. In t_1 the roundabout production commences when part of the labour potential is employed for the production of capital goods. In the subsequent periods it serves for the production of consumer goods. If we limit ourselves to country I, there are in period 2 for sector c_1 12 capital goods available, with the aid of which during period 28 c_1 can be produced. This requires 8 labour units. Consequently, during period 2 16 labour units still work in the c_1 sector of country I according to the original method of production. They produce 16 c_1, which leads to a total production of 44 c_1. This argument applies to each final product in each period and is analogous for the two countries.

Owing to the fact that in period I less labour is applied to the final product sector than before, but as production still takes place in accordance with the original techniques, the transformation curve – bearing in mind figure 20 – is still at a lower level than before.

Quoting Rostow, the main concern in this period is the fulfillment 'of the

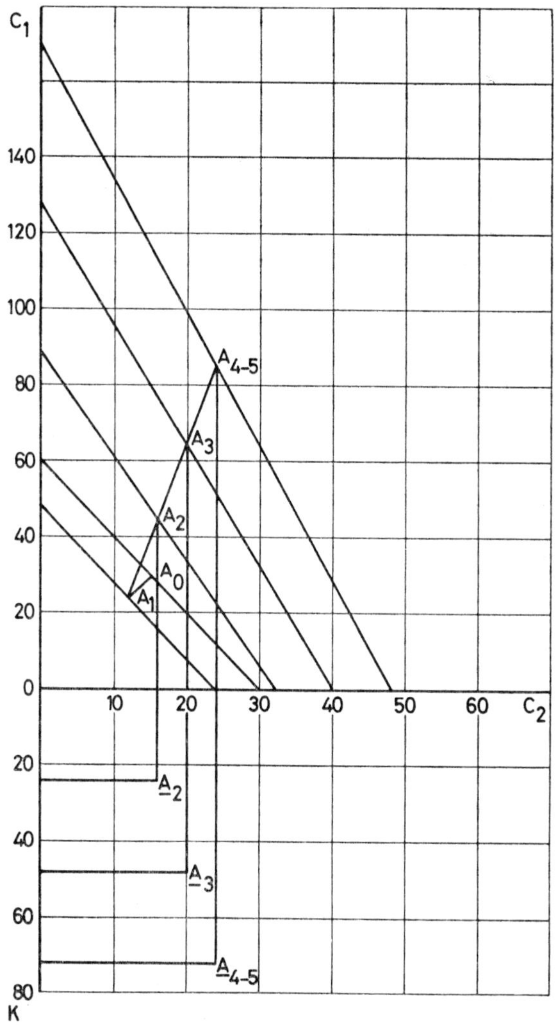

Fig. 20. Differentiated technical progress.

conditions for the start' for economic growth. In the next period the economic progress reached full growth and mass consumption. The situation is presented here in such a way that the technical progress is greatest in that sector in which the country concerned has already a comparative cost advantage. Table 11 therefore introduces economic growth with differentiated sectorial technical progress owing to the supposed drop of the labour coefficients (point 4).

All this means that in country I the production possibilities with regard to c_1 improve relatively. This is further expressed in the increasingly steeper transformation curves of figure 20. The points of tangency A^0 up to A^5 incl., based on the motivation given for this in the previous chapter, are once again precisely in the centre of the transformation lines. This has the effect that price ratios in an autarchic connection (point 5) develop to the detriment of the goods which can be produced under relatively more favourable circumstances. In the representation of figure 20 this is fairly clearly the case. After all, point A^0 to A^5 imply that half of the amount to be spent on consumer goods is always used for the purchase of one commodity – with regard to each of the goods there is an income elasticity of one –, which means that the real income growth is equal in the various sectors. The quantitative growth of disposal in the sector with the greatest technical progress, consequently coincides with a relative fall in price. Naturally this is disappointing as in this situation normal profit expectations are not realized.

This unpleasant development of the price ratios can be prevented by an extension of the geographic disposal area with production specialization and international trade. The price ratios then present a totally different picture. Points 6 and 7 of the previous row of eight must then be considered. This occurs in fact by the supposition that after reaching the autarchic equilibria in period 5 of table 11 – indicated by points A_5 (country I) and B_5 (country II) in figure 21 – the frontiers are opened. The optimum external exchange ratio is again indicated by the coinciding E_R lines of the individual countries. Production specialization and international trade, as indicated in table 11 and figure 21, are apparent and obvious from the above. Country I reaches a new equilibrium with D^1, country II reaches point E^1. This once again concerns the comparative cost theory in a pure form, there is no mixing of final product substitution.

The development of the price ratios – and this applies as a useful meaningful conclusion – now means that the initially relatively expensive becomes relatively cheaper and drops in price. After all, in country I c_2 becomes relatively cheaper and in country II c_1.

This provides a double advantage. Firstly, consumer demand is much better satisfied; secondly, the realisation of comparatively advantageous technical progress now also becomes interesting for the production sector concerned. After all, the relative drop in price of the commodity which can be produced comparatively cheaply, does not now occur. This indicates that

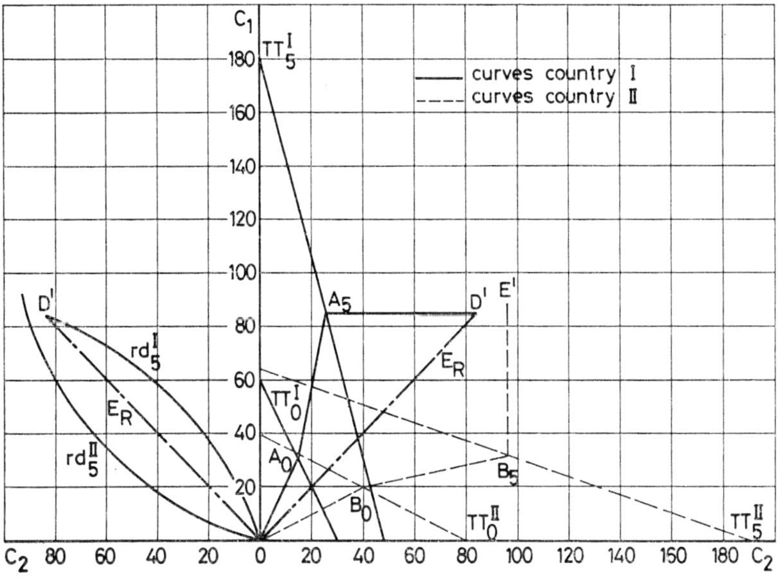

Fig. 21. The comparative cost theory and economic growth.

especially highly developed economies aim at production specialization and international trade.

Whereas in an undeveloped society the geographical areas of production and consumption more or less coincide, this does not appear to be the case in an economically developing economy. It is to be expected that there production will concentrate geographically, whereas consumption orientates itself on a worldwide scale.

Subsequently attention is drawn to income distribution or the last point of the above row of eight. This subject is quite extensive and we shall deal with it in a separate paragraph.

3. Setting in economic science

Income formation demands a good deal of attention as it requires another amendment of the neo-classic theory, namely with regard to the role of money. According to the neo-classical theory money has no independent meaning within the equilibrium framework, which caused the belief that there is a strict division between the price level as a subject for monetary science and the price ratios as a theme for value and price theory. So far we have implicitly accepted this opinion, as it is included in the equilibrium criteria used. After all, the simultaneous reaching of equilibrium at consumption and production so far proceeded in three stages with a fairly distinct neo-classical flavour:

- the criterion for the consumption sector was that the marginal utility ratio became equal to the reverse of the price ratio, as the marginal utilities of the last unit of money spent are equal to the purchase of c_1 or c_2 respectively. Such an optimum spending implies a maximization of the integral utility; after all the budget line then touches the highest achievable indifference curve. The question of what quantity of money is then in fact used need not explicitly be raised according to neo-classical opinion, because that is irrelevant with relation to reaching the equilibrium. After all, a doubling of that quantity will only lead to an increase of each individual price by 100%, without interfering with the price ratio. Consequently, a money quantity mutation has no independent influence on the consumption equilibrium scope. The observation resembles reality more closely when we assume a definite amount to be spent, based on which a budget line can be designed. This then requires knowledge of the nominal prices of the final products. The hyperbolic indifference curve helps in a calculation of this, as it aims at half the fixed amount of money in c_1 or c_2 respectively to be spent in equilibrium. It is then possible to design the budget line with its point of contact at the highest attainable indifference curve, precisely in the centre. This line of thought will be pursued further in the paragraph;
- The allocation of labour and capital will progress at equilibrium in such a way, that the required combination of final products required by the consumers is produced. Such a development is acceptable, as the optimum spending within the consumption sector and the allocation intended here together lead to a maximum earned income for the producers. A difficulty, however, is the precise description of 'earned income'. The neo-classical theory only presents the possibility of considering this income as the total consumptive utility, which reaches a maximum level at the point of contact of budget line and indifference curve. The motive for this theory may be that consumers and producers form personal unions, so that those offering bread or butter exchange until the slice is equally thick and equally well buttered. This theory appears to be acceptable for the 'Naturalwirtschaft' (barter economy). However, if roundabout production, exchange of goods, division of labour and the system of finance develop, it loses in reality value. In fact, the production sector then orientates itself towards

maximizing the amount of money received. This is not taken into account in the neo-classical theory, as according to this theory the demand for and the supply of goods, expressed in real prices, are equal for each economy and in every period. This representation means that each economy, during the period concerned, immediately adjust expenditure to receipts. Money and goods are demanded and offered and the value of these four (the demanded and offered money, and the demanded and offered goods respectively) are then realized together in time and are equal. Binswanger pointed out the untenability of this, because it is 'impossible for the single economy to adjust the amount of money which it offers on the one market, to the amount of money it demands on the other market...'.[1] Value and price formation consequently progress differently to what we are led to believe in the neo-classical theory. In reality, when I hand over a commodity with my left hand and receive money for it with my right, the value of the commodity passes to the money. Consequently for each individual operating on the market the values of money and the commodity do not arise simultaneously and in parallel; the money only acquires its value when the commodity is relinquished. Based on this it is desirable to consider the amount of money received by the production sector as 'earned income'. The explicit introduction of the money, which was decided just now, presents this possibility.

- The allocation possibilities for the production of the demanded final products can be indicated for each consumer commodity by an isoquant. Based on the given quantities of production means, these isoquants can be placed in an Edgeworth/Bowley diagram, when it becomes apparent that the required production is only possible at the point at which the lines concerned touch each other (points *A* and *B* in figure 18). The neo-classical theory considers this to be of decisive importance for income distribution, as in the point concerned, the marginal labour unit – in a similar way in the various sectors – receives a reward, which is equal to the replacing quantity of capital. This indicates an application of the marginal productivity theory. This appears to be a strong argument; after the earned income has reached a maximum level, there is such a balanced distribution, that nobody needs to be dissatisfied. A weak point in the theory is, that capital is then considered to be a given factor of production. This contains the danger that the theory will become too divorced from reality. With this in mind, we have ignored capital in this sense. Consequently, the question

1. H. C. Binswanger, *Markt und internationale Währungsordnung*. Pg. 46-50.

remains about the significance of the already indicated roundabout production, specialization and international trade for the distribution of income.

The above shows that from a neo-classical point of view only the price and income ratios – independent of the quantity of money and the price level – are relevant to the consumptive and productive equilibrium. This could be further explained with equation (9) in which

$$(9) \quad M = \frac{\varphi}{P} \left\{ \frac{p_{c1}}{p_{c2}} \right\}$$

M = the quantity of money
P = the price level
φ = an adjustment parameter

When M changes, this only leads to a change of P; in the event of mutation of the price ratios φ will adjust in such a way that M and P are not influenced. Methodologically speaking, a dichotomy is hereby accepted owing to the fact that there are two tenets – entirely independent – within one science. When answering the question whether this can indeed be the case within the economic process there is a remarkable difference. From a neo-classical point of view there are only immediately observable and strict logical relationships between the data, owing to which a dichotomy can be in accordance with reality. In opposition to this, the critical method, as designed in our 'Waardering van het economisch denken' is based on social-economic reality, in which everything is interdependent; data are lifted from this for the benefit of the theory. According to this point of view a dichotomy is never fundamental, but always the result of an abstracting data formulation. This general criticism of dichotomy already implicitly contains objections to the neo-classical views regarding the connection between price level and price rations, of the supposed significance of the quantity of money for the economic equilibrium respectively. This underlines the necessity to weigh carefully the neo-classical equilibrium analysis as already carried out – with a further introduction of money and capital as a derived production factor. To this purpose the stages described above will be considered once again. The consumption sector possesses a certain quantity of money to be spent, which enables the design of a budget line which touches in the centre the highest attainable indifference curve. The amount of money spent is subsequently the earned income for the producers, they aim at maximizing it.

Because capital as a problem does not permit an application of the marginal productivity theory, the problem of the income distribution must finally by investigated.

The first stage only briefly requires attention. Production specialization and international trade, according to table 11, are specified in table 12; they are brought about during the period 5 to 8 incl. Additionally, a possible further specialization and trade takes place in period 9. The theory is extended by the explicit introduction of the money by equation (10).

Table 12. Specialization of production and international trade.

	Production				Trade		Consumption			
	Country I		Country II				Country I		Country II	
t	c_1	c_2	c_1	c_2	c_1	c_2	c_1	c_2	c_1	c_2
5 (A_1^1, B_1^1)	84	24	32	96	–	–	84	24	32	96
6	112	16	$22\frac{2}{3}$	124	28	28	84	44	$50\frac{2}{3}$	96
7	140	8	$9\frac{1}{3}$	152	56	56	84	64	$69\frac{1}{3}$	96
8 (D_1, E_1)	168	–	4	180	84	84	84	84	88	96
9	168	–	–	192	112	112	56	112	112	80

Based on this the prices of the goods can be calculated after a certain given

$$(10) \quad M = C_1 \,.\, P_{c1} + C_2 \,.\, P_{cn}$$

quantity of money is pre-assumed in each country in period 5. Subsequently there is an accompaniment of the production specialization and the international trade in three different ways, in such a way that the monetary authorities keep the quantity of money:

- constant with as a result a deflationary specialization process;
- allow it to increase to such an extent that no price decreases occur, which causes inflationary specialization;
- allow it to grow in such a way that disposal of final products is possible at constant prices, owing to which specialization acquires a monetary-stable tendency.

In period 8 the consumption sector – as described in the previous paragraph – is in equilibrium; the question then is whether simultaneously the money income within the production sector reaches a maximum. Taking into account the different specialization processes, there is a theoretically stylized three-fold answer to this. The internal payment transaction, which is thereby introduced, takes place based on a rate of exchange (W_K), which is defined as follows:

$$W_K = \frac{C_1\text{-import of country II} \,.\, p_{c1}{}^{\mathrm{II}}}{C_2\text{-import of country I} \,.\, p_{c2}{}^{\mathrm{I}}}$$

This rate of exchange always provides a balance of payments equilibrium, as country I entirely exchanges the proceeds of the c_1-export for the proceeds of the c_2-export by country II. For reasons of simplicity, the international monetary transaction here does not independently influence the course of the economic process and can be further ignored.

The first monetary-political pattern in which the quantity of money remains constant in each country, is shown in table 13. Set against the above criterion – a simultaneous equilibrium – the entire process of the production sector is rather disheartening. After all, in country I there is the expectation that the c_1-export will be worthwhile, considering the high price in country II.

Table 13. Deflationary specialization process.

t	Country I Consumption					Country II Consumption				
	c_1	c_2	M	pc_1	pc_2	c_1	c_2	M	pc_1	pc_2
5	84	24	168	1	3,5	32	96	192	3	1
6	84	44	168	1	1,9	$50\frac{2}{3}$	96	192	1,9	1
7	84	64	168	1	1,3	$69\frac{1}{3}$	96	192	1,4	1
8	84	84	168	1	1	88	96	192	1,1	1

However, during each period the export brings such a fall in price that the expectations are not realized. Country II experiences the same disappointing result with the export of c_2. All this is a result of the quantitatively narrow monetary policy being pursued, directed towards 'control of the total size and composition of M with objects in the monetary sphere'.[2] This policy is characteristic of the gold standard, in which the 'control of the monetary system is ruled by an objective criterion, which is independent of general-political objectives and considerations'.[2] In fact, this meant 'That the primary objective of the monetary authorities consisted in the maintenance of the fixed gold price'. The constant quantity of money of table 13 then has as monetary-political background, the fact that the gold holding of the central bank does not change, and the rules of the gold standard are consequently applied. It is remarkable here that the price ratios exclusively change by price decrease of the commodity which is imported. Owing to this, the specialization process has a distinct deflationary character. For the production sector all this is not really to the point, and it is not surprising that production specialization and international trade have little chance of success with this monetary accompaniment.

2. S. Korteweg and F. A. G. Keesing, *Het moderne geldwezen*. Pg. 582 and 588 resp.

Until the end of the sixties the post-war international monetary system presented a different picture from the one described above. Within the framework of the Bretton Woods agreements there were stable exchange rates, whilst within the national boundaries a wide quantitative monetary policy was pursued, especially in connection with the tendency towards full employment.

Table 14. Inflationary specialization process.

	Country I Consumption					Country II Consumption				
t	c_1	c_2	M	pc_1	pc_2	c_1	c_2	M	pc_1	pc_2
5	84	24	168	1	3,5	32	96	192	3	1
6	84	44	308	1,8	3,5	$50\frac{2}{3}$	96	304	3	1,7
7	84	64	448	2,7	3,5	$69\frac{1}{3}$	96	416	3	2,2
8	84	84	588	3,5	3,5	88	96	528	3	2,7
9	56	112	784	7	3,5	112	80	672	3	4,2

After all, this policy concerns a 'control of the total and composition of M with aims outside the monetary sphere'. The pursuance of full employment is a brake on price decreases. After all, these lower the profit expectations and weaken the entrepreneur's activity. The monetary policy can be directed towards prevention of price decreases. All this is shown in the figures of table 14. Price ratios change now, as the commodity on which a country specializes becomes more expensive. Consequently, an increase in the price level occurs and the specialization process has an inflationary tendency. However, once again no simultaneous equilibrium is reached. In country I income still increases during period 9, whereas the consumption sector reached equilibrium in period 8.

As is shown above, the tendency of a specialization process is determined by the value ratio of the goods and the nature of the monetary policy.

The deflationary and inflationary specialization agreed in one point that in both the growth of the quantity of money did not depend on the above value ratio. In the first case the quantity of money remained constant; in the second it increased in such a way that no money price had to decrease.

The results of this were not very satisfactory. In both situations a simultaneous equilibrium was not brought about. The question which monetary type of policy accompany specialization and trade was therefore not answered. As a result the attention is now directed towards the monetary-stable specialization process. This differs essentially from the above, as here there is a relationship between the value ratio of the goods and the quantity of money. This implies that the tendency to equilibrium depends on the manner in which in the course of time specialization and trade are realized. A systematic discussion of this subject can take place by initially accepting the value relationship as permanent in the course of time. Additionally, it is for the time being sufficient only to work with country I without roundabout production; this has been done in table 15. The growth arises by the decrease of the labour coefficient c_1. In the situations *a* and *b* the consumer goods are complementary. Despite a differentiated technical process, it is striking that the price ratios remain equal and independent from the time, *M* increases to 80.

Table 15. Economic equilibrium in the course of time.

Data								Variables			
	t	αc_1	αc_2	$\varkappa$	L	M		c_1	c_2	pc_1	pc_2
No. Consumption sector	0	1	2	$\frac{1}{2}$	60	60		30	15	1	2
a complementary goods	1	$\frac{1}{2}$	2	$\frac{1}{2}$	60	80		40	20	1	2
b	1	$\frac{3}{4}$	2	$\frac{1}{2}$	60	68,6		34,3	17,15	1	2
	2	$\frac{1}{2}$	2	$\frac{1}{2}$	60	80		40	20	1	2
c Substitutable goods	1	$\frac{1}{2}$	2	$\frac{1}{4}$	60	90		60	15	$\frac{3}{4}$	3
d	1	$\frac{2}{3}$	2	$\frac{3}{8}$	60	75		45	15	0,833	2,5
	2	$\frac{1}{2}$	2	$\frac{1}{4}$	60	87,5		60	15	0,73	2,93

For goods which can be substituted the situation is different; this is drawn based on the hyperbolic indifference curve in *c* and *d*. A change in the relative consumer preference and a net increase of the commodity which can be produced technically more efficiently then go together and determine together the higher level of consumer demand, as well as the income for the production sector. Situation *c* contains a reflection of this within one period; then *M* rises to 90. If two periods are required – according to *d* – then the growth is limited to 87.5. It is therefore apparent that the growth of income with substitutable consumer goods also depends on the time within which this growth is realized. Owing to that the monetary-equilibrium specialization differs from the already discussed deflation and inflation.

The basic point of the time aspect here is the orientation from the recent past to the near future; it contains a closely related experience and expectation. When forming an idea regarding the value of goods we constantly proceed from the recent past, in which that value often already exists as a fact. Expressed in prices at which those goods are available, those values contain the expectation pattern, which is the foundation for fiduciary money. A normal fulfillment of these expectations is possible in principle with the indicated monetary equilibrium policy. In this point our consideration is in agreement with the 'Principle of price continuation', which means that fundamentally economic subjects with regard to their ideas on the required price formation, always orientate themselves from a nearby past.[3] As from this orientation the value of the goods is mostly already given, a monetary policy is acceptable in which the quantity of money increases with the net growth of the goods multiplied by their prices. This is clearly the case in situations *a* and *b* of table 15, as there the price ratios do not change in the course of time. However, this is a theoretical abstraction, which as a phase in the construction of the theory may have constructive meaning; however, in reality a certain amount of substitution is more obvious. Owing to this there will be room for changes in the price relationships, for which there will be a particular need in the event of differentiated technical progress. Situations *c* and *d* in table 15 express this. The price ratios of yesterday, together with the final product mutation of today as compared to yesterday, determine the quantity of money, which is required from a monetary equilibrium point of view. Within the scope of this quantity of money the new price ratios are determined in a combination between production and consumption, creating in the course of time a close relationship between the development of the price ratios and the growth of the quantity of money. The latter will increase faster as the economic growth materializes more quickly.

This theory can be applied to specialization and trade, the result of which can be seen in table 12. The path of the monetary-stable accompaniment can be seen in figures in table 16. Country I, which in accordance with the theory expressed in the last paragraph, limits specialization and trade, experiences consumptive equilibrium in period 8, when simultaneously the income of the production sector reaches a maximum. This proves that a monetary-stable accompaniment of specialization and trade does enables a simultaneous equilibrium. All this implies that the neo-classical theory regarding the relationship between the price ratios, the quantity of money and reaching simultaneous equilibrium cannot be sustained.

3. O. von Zwiedineck-Südenhorst, *Mensch und Wirtschaft*. Pg. 42.

Table 16. Monetary equilibrium and specialization process.

	Country I Consumption					Country II Consumption				
t	c_1	c_2	M	pc_1	pc_2	c_1	c_2	M	pc_1	pc_2
5	84	24	168	1	3,5	32	96	192	3	1
6	84	44	238	1,4	2,7	$50\frac{2}{3}$	96	248	2,44	1,27
7	84	64	292	1,74	2,3	$69\frac{1}{3}$	96	291	2,1	1,52
8	84	84	336	2	2	88	96	331	1,88	1,72
9	56	112	336	3	1,5	112	80	337	1,5	2,1

The description of the consumption equilibrium is then limited to the equality of the price ratio to the reverse of the utility ratio; this suffices because this equality implies utility maximization. The equilibrium in the production sector is brought about from a neo-classical point of view, when the costs of the marginal labour unit are equal to those of the compensating capital. This means an acceptance of the marginal productivity theory, which can, however, only have meaning as an explanation of income distribution. This is not sufficient within a highly developed economic process, as here the production sector in the first place aspires to a maximum monetary income. As long as the dichotomy is accepted concerning the quantity of money and the price ratios, this incomplete description of the productive equilibrium is accompanied by an inadequate monetary theory, in the sense that the required quantity of money is in principle independent from the price ratios. The theory of international trade, as developed above, led to the view that in this manner a simultaneous equilibrium could not be reached. This required a two-fold amendment of the neo-classical theory. In the first place a further description of the equilibrium in the production sector was required and – secondly – the introduction of monetary-stable production specialization and international trade. These two supplements theoretically enabled a simultaneous equilibrium to be reached. However, this does not complete the analysis; the income distribution now demands attention.

This takes place based on equations (11) to (14) incl.

$$(11)\quad M = [(1-\beta)L]\ p_1 + I_{pi} + K_r{}^W$$

$$(12)\quad I_{pi} = (\beta L)\, p_l$$

$$(13)\quad \Delta K^W = I_{pi} - D^W$$

$$(14)\quad D^W = \left\{\frac{I_{pi}}{T}\right\}_{-t_1} + \dots + \left\{\frac{I_{pi}}{T}\right\}_{-t_n} \quad \text{in which:}$$

p_1 = the reward of a labour unit, which comes about in the c_1, the c_2 or the *i*-sector. We assume wage levelling, so that symbol p_1 suffices;

K^W = the acquisition value of the capital goods supply in use;

r = a fraction, in which K^W is multiplied for the calculation of the capital profitability;

D^W = the amount of depreciation.

In the final product sectors, and in accordance with (11), the money received is spent on wages, on capital goods which are bought and paid for during the production period, plus the capital profitability. Additionally, in equation (12) the price formation of the capital goods has been shown; in accordance with the supposition that in the investment sector only labour is applied, the proceeds are entirely a reward of this labour. Finally, in (13) and (14) the value of the capital goods in use and the depreciations have been defined. Suffix $-t_1$ refers to the preceding period and $-t_n$ to the life of the capital goods. Consequently, the series $-t_1, \ldots.., -t_n$ includes the number of periods during which a capital good can be applied for the production of final products. There are four equations and five unknown quantities, the latter being p_1, p_i, r, K^W and D^W.

This leads to the conclusion that within the economic theory, the income distribution can only be described hypothetically, which can be explained with the aid of equation (15), by which, for reasons of brevity, the income formation only within the c_2 sector has been indicated; see also figure 22.

$$(15) \quad C_2 \cdot p_{c2} = (\varepsilon L)p_1{}^{c2} + (\beta L)p_1{}^{i} + K^W{}_{c2}r.$$

The price sum is shown by line section *0A*. In the absence of capital return the wages sum is *0C*. When subsequently the wages in the final product and in the investment sector are equal, then the economic process takes place in a special manner. The workers see technical possibilities, save voluntarily on wages in the final product sector in order to pay their colleagues, who in mutual consultation have been pushed forward in the production column – all very peacefully. However, we have already seen that the western economy has developed differently. This point clearly shows that economic science must not disassociate itself from the lines of historical development.

Using the technical possibilities, the entrepreneur/capital provider has in the application of labour for the production of capital goods provided complementary monetary savings, but only with a specific capital return as re-

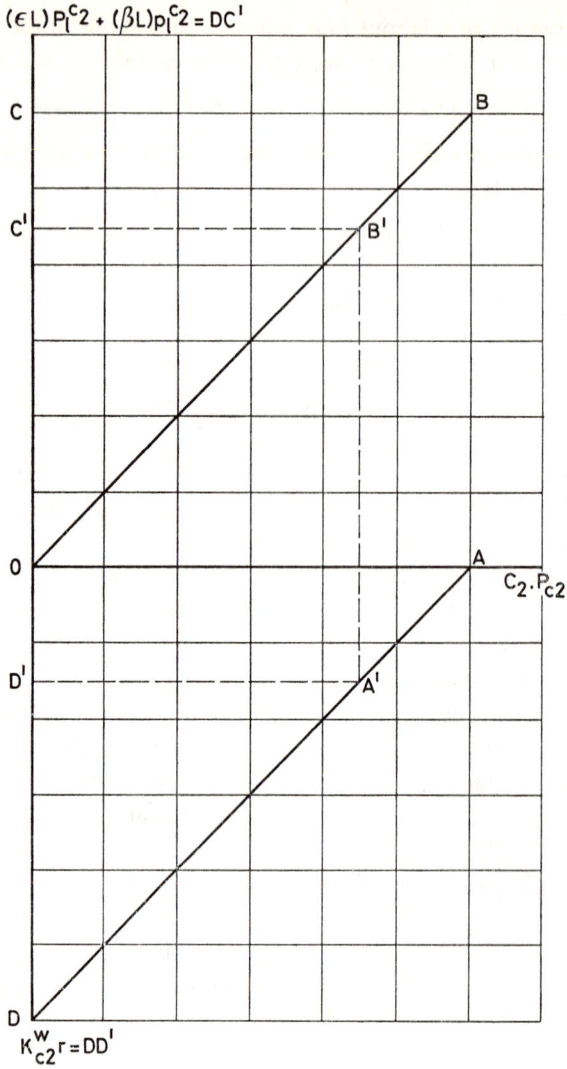

Fig. 22. The formation of income and roundabout production.

ward for his efforts. In the resulting income formation, the wage ratio between the various stages in the production column plays an important part. Assuming a tendency towards levelling of wages, the interest does not only provide equilibrium between the demand for and the supply of savings, there is additionally a link between wages in the final product and in the capital goods sector. One may hope that the relationship between the reward of labour and capital leads to full employment, a stable distribution of labour between the final product and the capital goods sector, plus a stable price level. The economic theory cannot guarantee this, it can only conclude that the income distribution in the industrial society – with production specialization and international trade – is a field of social forces, from which deviations from the above situation may arise. Consequently, owing to hypotheses, that theory covers a more limited field than the social-economic reality and the realisation of the theoretically formulated equilibrium is a relative matter.

The above leads to the conclusion that the marginal productivity theory is inadequate; it is too limited concerning data determination. It assumes that the demand for and the supply of the means of production are immediately given; income formation is a consequence of the market process, with the result that each production factor is rewarded in accordance with its marginal productivity. John Bates Clark considers this as a standard: 'A plan of living that should force men to leave in their employers' hand anything that by right of creation is theirs, would be an institutional robbery – a legally established violation of the principle on which property is supposed to rest'.[4] This neo-classical approach has three characteristics. In the first place it is based on some simple, apparently obvious principles, such as given production means and an aspiration for minimum costs; c.q. a maximum return. This implies – secondly – a social structure which is clearly liberally based, with strict individual property rights and free contract making. Finally, the economic process must be realized in such a way, that this society concept is practically realized. Besides Clark's opinion regarding income distribution, the enforced gold standard illustrates this.

Clark's theory has never been positively accepted; yet the thought that come what may income distribution progresses in accordance with the marginal productivity theory has taken root. This is apparent from the treatment of the income theory in economic-theoretical works. For example, Lipsey and Steiner[5] state that within our society the reward to a factor of production is based on its marginal production and on this organisations such as the trade union movement, can make but little impact.

According to the same authors, the scientific criticism of the marginal productivity theory is not acceptable. The progress of economic processes in general and income distribution in particular are determined in this theory by fundamental irregularities in the social life with a scientific character. In fact then, there is freedom for economic action in only one direction. Above

4. John Bates Clark, *The Distribution of Wealth*. Pg. 9.
5. Richard G. Lipsey and Peter O. Steiner, *Economics*. Pg. 327-403.

we have divorced ourselves from this view, and consequently have a picture of economic science as such, and the place of international economics within it, which differs considerably from the neo-classical concepts. This can be further explained with the aid of the four methodological basic points, which have already been mentioned at the end of the last chapter:

– the difference in intention in the practice of science. This is apparent from the choice of data, which according to the neo-classical method takes place at the boundary of criticism and theory. Owing to this data are simple and obvious, not requiring discussion: 'They are so much the stuff of our every day experience that they have only to be stated to be recognized as being obvious'.[6] Such data are directly and uniformly described as the basis for the theoretical analysis. The economic process is then a priori a strictly-logically ordered unit and the scientific intention aims at providing in principle complete information about this; the smallest details of a strictly-rationally ordered object of study can after all be further traced by an ever deepening mathematical analysis. A recent study by Batra clearly indicates that this method forms the foundation of the present theory of international trade.[7] The theory then develops by calculating work which becomes increasingly difficult with refinement of the graphical representations, and more detailed mathematical models. The economic process is then hypothetical – owing to a physically approach – full of thoughts given for us; the task of science is to analyse these. The critical method is different in nature; the economic process occurs as a result of multisided human initiative and consequently, it is full of our own thoughts which leads to a two-fold difference. In the first place the choice of data now no longer occurs at the boundary of criticism and theory, but by an appraisal of the prevailing social-economic order. The data are then removed from reality and formulated later at the boundary of criticism and theory in a logical form. Secondly, the study of economics is then not directed towards studying the economic processes as an assumed strictly logical entity, but towards finding a theoretically satisfactory solution to problems which we formulate by critical assessment. This difference became apparent in the description of capital as datum, or as a problem respectively. In neo-classical thinking that production factor was a given component for a closed equilibrium theory; for the critical method, capital is a problem for reflection of – among others – growth and income problems;

6. L. Robbins, *An Essay on the Nature and Significance of Economic Science*. Pg. 79.
7. R. N. Batra, *Studies in the Pure Theory of International Trade*.

– the relativity of the freedom of value. Neo-classical thinking is fairly explicitly based on the concept of a liberal society. The methodological feature is closely related to the data choice, based on the individualistic 'homo economicus' only aspiring after utility and profit maximization. Owing to this the scientist has no room for social judgements on his own initiative, the classical theory only offers him a freedom in one direction with regard to ideas about society. Here too there is a difference with the critical method, as according to the latter the economy based on freedom of value cannot develop satisfactorily. Critical evaluation results in a social ideology; this contains a central value complex with regard to the structure of society. The ideology concerned is of an analytical or of a critical nature. In the first case the social criticism starts from the conviction that there is an ideal-social order in theory, away from place and time. The second form of social-ideological thinking includes an historically based critical approach of the existing society. Up to the thirties the western economy – and in particular the neo-classical method – was based on a liberal-individualistic ideology, and that is still mainly the case, in so far as it concerns the theory of international trade. Within economic science much has changed since Keynes on this point. This results in the western economy being at the moment – grosso modo – indifferent to analytical social ideologies. However, this does mean that the data determination still takes place at the boundary of criticism and theory. Consequently, current economic thought still does not methodologically permit a reflective-appreciative thinking based on the critical ideology.

So far it is not value-free. There is dissatisfaction about this, as the analytical ideology as a form of social criticism did fit in former days, but does not do so any longer. At present there is a need for an assessing reflective approach, by which we now come to judge our criticism of yesterday. If there is methodologically room for it, the critical ideology and method are accepted. As is apparent from the above there is a need for that within the theory of international trade;

– the different relationship between micro and macro economics or the difference in interpretation of the economic equilibrium respectively. From a neo-classical point of view, a simultaneous equilibrium is reached entirely within a micro framework, leaving only room for a descriptive macro economy. This equilibrium is rooted in the liberal social ideology, which is analytical in nature. Owing to this the equilibrium criteria have a liberal individualistic tendency and contain the pretence of being solely infallible. Based on the pre-supposed freedom in one direction, the neo-classical equilibrium says of itself that it must be realized. The formulation of the equilibrium criteria in the indicated manner means that only price and income ratios can be considered relevant; the quantity of money and the price level do not play a decisive part. This appears to be acceptable for 'Naturalwirtschaft', but within a developed economy one must have at least a re-formulation in the sense that the production sector there aspires to a maximum monetary income. The described social-ideological foundation prevents such a re-formulation for the neo-classical theory; consequently, it maintains the opinion that a production factor is rewarded in accordance with its marginal product. Additionally, it retains a monetary theory – in principle the gold standard –[8] by which the growth of the quantity of money does not depend on the development of the price ratios. The result of this is a dichotomy, within the framework of which – and entirely removed from one another, the price ratios are a subject for value and the price theory and the general price level forms a theme for the monetary theory. This dichotomy is a basic point in the neo-classical methodology. That it cannot be maintained becomes clearly obvious within the comparative cost theory. When the equilibrium in the production sector is re-written as the aspiration to a maximum money income, the neo-classical monetary basic point – as is apparent from the theory of the comparative costs – does no present the possibility of reaching a simultaneous equilibrium within the different sectors of the various countries. A solution of this problem begins by ignoring the indicated dichotomy, which has been done principally methodologically in the design of the critical method. A monetary equilibrium point of beginning, in the sense that the quantity of money grows with the net increase of the goods multiplied by their prices, enables a harmonious connection between the development of the price ratios, the growth of the quantity of money and reaching a simultaneous equilibrium. However, this means that the liberal analytical society conceptions have been left behind; instead the critical ideology has been accepted. This is apparent because the equilibrium as such has acquired another meaning. It is no longer a rule which must be realized, almost of necessity, but a critically assessed social economic objective which is worth aiming at. The theoretical reflection of the realisation of this has micro and macro aspects, both of which – in so far as they are useful and necessary – will have a place in this study;

8. See also our study *Economische orde en Europese monetaire integratie*. Chapter II, para 1.

– the different opinions regarding the historic dependency of economic thinking. The neo-classical method places economic science methodically outside history. The choice of the data directly on the boundary of criticism and theory means that this is 'timeless', in the sense that the contents of the data are not dependent on historical influences. Additionally, the analytical ideology contains a picture of an ideal society removed from time and place. Finally, the neo-classical equilibrium aims at a somewhat forceful realisation irrespective of the historical situation. Based on these fundamental points economic science only concerns itself in a three-fold way with theoretical time. It is static (the analysis concerns the situation at a specific moment), comparatively static (a comparison of the situation at different moments without anything else) or dynamic (when also the course of events between the moments is described). It always concerns theoretically programmed time, during which hypothetical events materialize. However, in reality the economic process takes place in historical time. When it is intended that economic science should contribute towards the required progress of that process, it is undesirable to separate it methodologically from history. A possibility for the required connection, with the necessary changes in the choice of data, the social ideology and the equilibrium criteria – is offered by the critical method. In the above this has formed the foundation to the theory of international trade and it seems as if such a determination of place within economic science meets a need.

The essential difference between the neo-classical and the critical method concerns freedom in scientific pursuits. In this connection, it is desirable to make a distinction between freedom as such and the use of it. Whereas the nature of freedom may always remain hidden from us, we have a need for the use of freedom, even in science. However, it is possible that in doing so we use freedom in such a way that it disappears at once. Future scientific thinking then only includes theoretical-rational equilibrium movement. In the application of the neo-classical method, this is fairly clearly the case. Then data are chosen in such a way that a change of these at a later date will not take place in principle. The acceptance of an analytical social ideology means a statement of agreement as to future social freedom in one direction. And the equilibrium which must be more or less forcefully achieved leaves no room for renewed initiative in the future. The critical method is different in nature at these three points. It selects the data within a historical social-economic context, which leaves the possibility of later re-formulation. Furthermore, the critical ideology leads in principle not to a freedom in one direction, as this may change in content in the course of time because of its historical connection. Additionally, equilibrium although being a social economic objective worth aiming at, there is no guarantee that it will actually be reached, when there is the possibility of a change in content. That is why a theory of international trade based on the critical method does not form a complete unit, it is open in the sense that there is always the possibility of introducing problems, which we formulate when thinking critically.

EVALUATION

At the end of our study we return to the beginning. The question which concerns us is, to what extent the described theoretical model of international trade is acceptable and can withstand criticism. It has – as well as the introduction to this book – a methodological object. Formulating a reply by evaluation means a reflective re-thinking of what was undertaken for the construction of that model. Such a consideration of the nature and tendency of scientific work – a re-thinking in the correct meaning of the word – has as its starting point the assumption that the preceeding is of a two-fold nature; it includes criticism and theory. This is justified because economic science can only develop when based on those two. Critical thinking as an indispensable beginning, whilst observing and assessing, then aims at reaching a logical data description from the social economic reality. Further to this, it is the task of theory to discover and formulate rational regularities in economic action based on the described data and the recognized rules for a logical analysis. It can be concluded from these different modes of thinking that reflective re-assessment of criticism and theory can take place in two stages. In the first place it can examine to what extent the data have been distilled in a responsible manner from the social-economic reality; secondly, a strictly-logical assessment of the theoretical mode of thinking is required.

In this study the society-critical and formally-logical point of view assumed here for the construction of a theoretical model of international trade, actually forms a beginning, but in fact they were not always as clearly defined as indicated here. The two opinions were practically combined in the question whether the data, which have been accepted in different stages of the theory of international trade, offered the possibility of a rounded sensible theoretical analysis within the framework of a good problem posing. This latter always included the three-fold question on which basis of external exchange ratio, at which degree of production specialization and at which size of international trade simultaneous equilibrium can be reached, in the sense that for none of the participating countries is there a reason for executing changes in the decisions regarding the progress of the economic process. A satisfactory reply to the three-fold question posed is only possible with a theoretical analysis based on a specific, set of data, which is micro and macro economically well-formulated, in which production and consumption are wholly realistically included. The point of view from which the analysis was constructed was therefore the question whether normal conditions in the data description have so far been met. A review of the variations in the theory of international trade since Ricardo led to the conclusion that this is not the case. Simultaneously, it also became apparent in the above chapters what the contents of the above set of data, in fact, can be in so far as it concerns both production and consumption. In accordance with a three-fold differentiation the means of production are:

- not-re-allocatable and can then only be used for the production of the one or the other commodity;
- either original, at least quantitatively given and re-allocatable;
- or re-allocatable, when – assuming two factors of production – the one is original and the other derived.

The first case can be put theoretically with the supposition that a product is only produced in one country. Given the size and the technical suitability of the production factors the production for each country can then be indicated with a point on the y or on the x axis. In the second and third cases it is possible for the description of the production possibilities to construct transformation lines, either concave or not, which has always been done. Additionally, it is possible to indicate the relationships within the consumption sector based on a hyperbolic indifference curve, which has the property that the product of the co-ordinates is constant. In this study, this course has always been followed with the main consideration that in this way the theoretical analysis is simplified in a reasonable fashion.

The described variations in production and consumption relationships clearly require that the external exchange ratio, the degree of production specialization and the size of international trade is investigated in three different situations, depending on the nature of the factors of production and the concrete situation of the indifference curves. The completion of this programme, which is rather extensive at first sight, is less difficult than the first impression suggests, owing to an attractive uniformity in the variety.

This means that in the concrete analysis the same four-fold graphical set of instruments can be constantly used, which we shall now number a), b), c) and d). In this connection, a) the production points on the y and x axis, or the transformation lines respectively, plus b) the indifference curves are al-

alysis of international trade theory.

Equilibrium criteria uation oduction sector	a External exchange ratio	b Specialization of production	c International trade
The means of production cannot be re-allocated.	The optimum external exchange ratio is represented in three different situations in some way, normally by the coincidence of *ER*-curves of the	Specialization of production is impossible; production already occurs in a special direction in the autarchic situation.	International trade causes substitution of final products. The theory of comparative costs does not apply.
The means of production are, originally, or – at least – quantitatively given and can be re-allocated.	participating countries and additionally concretely on these curves bij the point of intersection of the *ER* and the *rd*-line nearest the origin.	Specialization of production is possible, however, without correct introduction of economic growth.	International trade and specialization of production cause a increase of the relative expensive product.
		Methodologically this is on application of the neo-classical approach. There is no satisfactory link with the theory of economic growth and the income theory breaks down in an application of the mergical productivity theory.	
Of two re-allocatable productions means, one is original and the other derived.		Specialization of production is now possible with a correct introduction of economic growth.	There is also a net increase of the relatively expensive commodity.
		By ignoring the neo-classical method capital can be introduced as a variable for economic theory, whereas distribution of income can be considered as a problem for social economic policy.	

ready mentioned in this evaluation. To this only c) the 'reciprocal demand' and d) the external exchange ratio line need be added. There is a close theoretically important relationship between c) and d).

Actually, the '*rd*' line forms a cost curve for the indication of the quantity of a specific commodity which a country is prepared to dispose of for a specific quantity of another commodity. Additionally, the E_R-curve is a proceeds line, which indicates whether the country concerned can really acquire the demanded quantity of that other commodity. The two curves in relationship to one another show in this way to what extent international trade is a proposition for the country concerned; as soon as the lines intersect, the costs and proceeds are equal, beyond that point trade across the frontiers creates a loss.

Naturally, many '*rd*'- and corresponding E_R-lines can be designed for each country but only one E_R-curve will coincide with that of the other country. Based on that communal E_R-line production specialization and international trade is possible to mutual advantage. This can be seen in the attached 'analyses'. All this implies with relation to the usual theory of international trade four modifications:

a. The Ricardian approach is based on the labour theory of value; however, this is not a good basis for the theory of comparative costs for two reasons. In the first place this theory indicates the advantages, which are achieved with production specialization and international trade, in the form of labour saving. The possibility to reduce labour saving of the individual countries comparatively to the same denominator fails here. This results in the fact that only the boundary between relative and absolute exploitation can be given, but not the international economic equilibrium. Additionally, the labour saving criterion – when we reach the second objection – is inadequate, as in fact, the saving to be calculated does not take place. The use of advantages presented by the existence of comparative cost differences is expressed in a net increase of the relatively expensive commodity. Considering these two objections, the Ricardian theory can be interpreted with labour as the sole scarce production factor. In this most positive case it does not form more than the introduction to a micro-economic technical production condition for the existence of comparative cost differences. This is inadequate data determination;

b. Mill, Marshall and Edgeworth following Ricardo endeavoured to indicate the optimum exchange ratio within the framework of the comparative cost theory by the 'equation of international demand' and by 'reciprocal demand curves'. By this, they implicitly introduced the production factor in such a way that international trade takes place without re-allocation of production. This manner of examination also falls short, because clearly the description of the production sector requires a choice, the factors of production cannot be re-allocated, as they can only be used for the production of a specific commodity, or the individual countries already have a specialized production before opening their frontiers.

In the first case the comparative cost theory does not apply, in the second situation there was already specialized production before the start of the analysis, whereas the comparative cost theory concerns itself with discovering whether and to what extent such a specialization will be decided upon. Naturally, only the first interpretation is scientifically acceptable; this is why for the construction of a theoretical model of international trade the theory of Mill c.s. is outside the comparative cost theory. The construction of external exchange ratio suits given production factors which cannot be re-allocated, and international trade by substitution of final products, which has been mentioned in 1 of the analysis;

c. according to Heckscher and Ohlin, international trade is a result of differentiated availability of production factors from country to country, from region to region respectively. This approach provides the possibility of completing the incomplete Ricardian data set with macro data and the consumption sector. It is usual to work out Heckscher and Ohlin's theory in a graphical manner with indifference curves and concave transformation lines, in order to solve on that basis the three basic questions of the comparative cost theory. The theoretical purity of this can be questioned, as international trade after all appears to be a form of mixing final product substitution and the use of advantages hidden in the existing comparative cost differences. For a methodologically correct description of the external exchange relationship, the production specialization and the trade across the frontiers within the framework of comparative cost theory, it is necessary to eliminate final product substitution. The possible result of this is shown in situation 2 of the analyses;

d. if the analysis does not proceed beyond the original, at least the given production factors which can be re-allocated, then it breaks down in an application of the neo-classical method. The inclination to this is quite pronounced. In fact, this is expressed in the extension of the theory of international trade based on concave transformation curves in the direction of economic growth and income distribution with the 'factor price equalisation'. As for the introduction of this manner of economic growth, two important shortcomings can be pointed out. In the first place capital formation remains un-explained and that is methodologically unacceptable; secondly, the theory deteriorates into a practically endless scientifically uninteresting casuistry. Furthermore, the introduction of income formation is faulty, as this breaks down in the marginal productivity theory. In fact, the two-fold extension of the comparative cost theory – i.e. in the direction of economic growth and income distribution – is only possible with capital as a problem in accordance with situation 3 of analyses, with all the limitations attached to it.

From this four stage development it can be deduced that within the theory of international trade, with relation to the production sector, a distinction is necessary between the situations in which re-allocation is possible or not. In the first instance, in which re-allocation is excluded such as, for instance, in which re-allocation is excluded such as, for instance with mono-cultures the theory remains limited to a description of the optimum external exchange ratio and the size of international trade; production specialization ex hypothesi is not relevant. The description of exchange ratio concerned and trade based on the above four curves took place in chapters III and IV. It appeared to be possible to introduce economic growth in a equilibrium manner.

In the second situation, in which re-allocation of production factor is possible, the comparative cost theory applies. Capital can then be assumed as given or as of problematic magnitude, and consequently, as capable of explanation in scientific terms. The analysis with capital as a given production factor was once again extensively dealt with. In the light of the above remarks sub *c* regarding the theoretical elaboration of the Heckscher/Ohlin principle, it was necessary to solve the three fundamental questions of the comparative cost theory – consequently without mixing with the final product substitution – within the framework of this principle. The already described four-fold graphical arrangement showed the possibility of this, which was used in para 1 of chapter VI. The result was disappointing, as the data description which forms the foundation of it all, has but little practical significance. Additionally, the field of vision remained methodologically limited. If the theory of international trade does not go beyond a study based on given factors of production, it remains limited to the Heckscher/Ohlin principle and an application of the neo-classical method. This distills its data without critical thinking, observing and assessing from social-economic reality, but formulating them directly on the boundary of criticism and theory. Strictly-logical relationships are pre-supposed between these data. This implies scientific-philosophically a value-free economic process placed outside history as a rationally ordered totality. This method contains the pretence of being able to describe economic events in the greatest detail – which are always strictly logical in nature. The theory then offers in principle complete information regarding the progress of the economic process, which can be indicated with an ever continuing mathematical specialization. To an increasing extent this method proves to be inadequate. The required revision can take place in principle with the introduction of capital as a magnitude to be explained, which, in fact, can take place by considering the production factor concerned as 'vorgetane Arbeit'. This means an approach to capital formation comes in its historical context with especially the tension between entrepreneurs and capital providers on the one hand and the working group on the other. Additionally, with capital in the manner indicated, international trade and economic growth can be related more efficiently than in earlier situations, as particularly from developed economies endeavours will be made to find extensions of the geographical field for the disposal of final products. The solution of the three fundamental problems of comparative cost theory progresses with capital formation as a problem analytically in the same manner as in the already described situations. When discussing income formation and distribution the necessity to break away from the neo-classical method became obvious owing to an inadequate formulation of the equilibrium criteria. The concept that in this connection it is sufficient to assume that each production factor receives a reward in accordance with its marginal productivity, had to be reviewed; this meant that the supposed dichotomy regarding the price ratios and the price level was untenable. The formulation of the equilibrium in the production sector was adjusted, in the sense that within the sector concerned a maximum monetary income is pursued.

A simultaneous equilibrium in production and consumption is then only possible if the production specialization and the international trade are accompanied by monetary stability, owing to the fact that the quantity of money grows with the net increase of the goods multiplied by their prices. This implies a close relationship between the quantity of money and the price ratios, which, in principle enables the simultaneous reaching of economic equilibrium. However, income distribution then remains an economic-political area of forces. With the construction of this theory the neo-classical method has in fact already made way for the critical method, with implications regarding:

- the data determination. Based on a critical assessment the data are abstracted from the social-economic reality and subsequently formulated logically on the boundary of criticism and theory for the benefit of the theoretical analysis;
- the freedom of value. The critical social ideology was accepted, which by nature is a assessment of the prevailing social-economic order for a particular period. The idea regarding an ideal theoretical society is thereby in principle left behind;
- the relationship between micro and macro economy. Science pre-supposes

the economic process to be no longer a strictly rationally ordered unit which it must describe mathematically. It is its task to seek for theoretically justified solutions to problems which we formulate after critical assessment. A micro or macro study is ensued whichever is suitable or necessary for the treatment of the subject;

– the relationship of economic science to history. The historical relationship of the economic process is no longer denied, but forms a methodological corner stone for a correct adjustment of criticism and theory.

The essential difference is that in the application of the neo-classical method economic science with regard to reality is theoretically closed, whereas it is always open when accepting the critical method of analysis of problems, which we formulate from critical assessment. Our study contains no more than a beginning for a revision of the theory of international trade based on this methodological re-orientation.

SYNOPSIS „VALUATION OF ECONOMIC SCIENCE"

There is an increasing concern about the inadequacy of the usual economic-scientific method, which is concretely expressed in recent architectonic and neo-marxian criticism. The first form, which is exercised by Mishan, Tinbergen, Boulding and Galbraith aims at the evolutionary but fairly extensive improvement of the economic system. The established economic order is sharply rejected by the recent revolutionary neo-marxian reservations. The core of the problem is correctly given by Myrdal. It consists of the fact that the present economy in the western world claims to be free of value. However, this claim is not tenable, as practising economic science always includes a certain appreciation of the economic process. The relating practice of science is after all, directed towards the establishment of rationally justified solutions to problems in connection with the allocation of the factors of production, which we are occupied in assessing. This valuation has methodological consequences, which so far have been inadequately recognized, because, erroneously, the postulate of the freedom of value is more or less common property.

The extent to which the present economic science is methodologically characterized by a social-assessment which forms its foundation, can be shown to be based on a description of the nature of the social criticism. This is always expressed in the form of a social ideology, which we consider as being the central value complex for the formation of society. There are two possibilities for the manner in which that criticism is established. It can be realized in an analytical, or in a critical ideology. In the first instance it contains an indication of the ideal theoretical society which is assumed – removed from place and time – as THE ideal worthy of aspiration. In the second situation ideology is a reflective assessment of the existing society, which means therefore that its contents is bound to place and time. As for practical social-economic life this distinction may appear to be somewhat sharp; however, for a description of the method of how the economy works, it is instructive and indispensable.

The distinction is of considerable importance to an assessment of economic science, as it leads to the conclusion that this science in its present form is not free of value; it is only indifferent to analytical ideologies. Analytical thinking does not permit the economy to develop within its frontiers, to this purpose it has shut itself off. This implies that economic science, as we know it at the moment, cannot claim to be value free. All this is fairly evident from four methodological characteristics of the economic science in its present construction, which are a direct result of the indicated social-ideological preference. The economic science is at the moment:

- based on independent data, which additionally must be described in a uniform manner and between which there must only be strictly logical relationships. This is in accordance with the methodological requirements of analytical ideology, which, however, implies that within the boundaries of economic science only a strictly logical and consequently only a similar reflective assessment is possible;
- characterized by the application of large scale mathematical methods. This is understandable – even obvious – as the system of data choice, implies that the economic process is analytically accepted as a strictly rationally ordered totality; which in principle, can be entirely mathematically proved;
- macro and micro analytically based on efficiency considerations. It is not possible to comprehend a highly developed economic process as a strictly-logically ordered totality at once. The macro approach serves for a rough description of the economic process. The micro analysis provides the detailed information;
- timeless, in the sense that the economic process at which the analysis is directed, is placed hypothetically outside history. The process concerned is theoretically a matter which is independent of place and time.

This four-fold methodological construction is historically understandable. It originates from Alfred Marshall, who as far back as in 1885 stated that economics must not be considered as being a 'body of concrete truth', but as 'an engine for the discovery of concrete truth'. Marshall reached the same conclusion by a critical study of the method of the classics – in particular of Ricardo – according to whom the economic process would be governed by laws of physical science.

This methodological development within the economy of the classics, according to Marshall, and subsequently, right up to the present, took place in a parallel manner within the positivistic philosophy of science. In accordance with the opinions of the classical school, the old positivists held the opinion that science always aims at recording completely certain knowledge.

The motive for this was that – if no complete certain knowledge is acquired – we do not know anything for certain. Popper, like Marshall, only a little later, criticized this philosophy of science with critical rationalism. This has the tendency that science is always directed towards the acquisition of empirical, epistemological insight. The knowledge acquired is therefore relative, it can only be upheld as long as it is not qualified as untenable by rational analysis. This theory of science is concretely applied within the present economy. However, it is also the economic science in accordance with this methodological construction, to which the above criticism is directed.

The dissatisfaction is understandable and in principle acceptable, as the analytical ideology of social criticism is suitable to an even lesser extent. Admittedly, until recently social criticism emphasised the method by which society must be ordered, without reference to the specific historical situation. However, this mainly belongs to the past. Even though a complete transfer has not yet happened, it is apparent that the critical ideology is gaining in importance.

A fundamentally critical approach to society always has two aspects. In the first instance it indicates a specific assessment of the existing society and secondly it indicates – with or without a great deal of vision – what changes must be executed. The social criticism with this two-fold aim was in the past and is at the present prevailing in a different manner. Formerly social criticism was mainly concerned from the point of view of its contents, without recognizing it as a phenomenon.

The emphasis was to indicate areas of dissatisfaction, and those changes to be executed based on principle considerations. A specific hypothetical society was postulated as an ideal based on certain principles – including those of a christian, liberal, socialistic or communistic nature. This is no longer so. Criticism, at least at first sight, lost its principle-firm attraction and became a more practical determination of a point of view based on efficiency considerations and self interest. This indicates a changed vision of social criticism as a phenomenon with far-reaching consequences. The fundamental fact is that whoever tries to describe how society should, in fact, be constructed without reference to time and place, puts himself beyond the social realities, whereas only from this social perspective with possibilities of realisation construction can take place. All this contains the question about the nature of social criticism as a phenomenon. The analytical ideology does not present a satisfactory reply to this. The criticism was moulded in such a form, that a reflective assessment, if it was not based on strict logic, was excluded at a later point of time. Consequently, it lacks something essential, it does not contain an indication of the time during which its subject matter is applicable. There will be resistance to such a limitation. After all, each generation is confronted with the task of constructing society in accordance with the requirements laid down by the historical situation in which it finds itself.

The social criticism of earlier days does not present this opportunity, as it claims to offer each new generation a ready made programme. However, this is not in accordance with the nature of social ideology, as this always contains an approximation of existing social-economic relationships, which will change its nature as society changes. It can be concluded from this nature of the social ideology that only to a limited degree does it point to the real future society. As a critical approximation of the existing society, it is always subjected to change. After all, one step in the direction of society as desired, changes the reality and as such the view of the desired society. The perspective of the social ideologies – especially when it contains a view towards the only correct society – never becomes completely realistic; it is an ever changing kaleidoscope. As soon as something in the perspective has been changed, reality changes and so does the perspective.

An important source of architectonic and neo-marxian reservations is that to an increasing extent the social criticism divorces itself from the traditional analytical form, whereas methodologically hardly anything can yet be observed within economic science. This situation raises the question for an assessment of economic thinking as to whether it is really desirable that the economy is subjected to a methodological change in the sense that the analytical ideology as a foundation is relinquished, in exchange for which the critical ideology can be accepted.

In the first place it may be noted that the changes in social criticism – for the time being ignoring the methodological consequences – create a complex problem for those experiencing and executing the changes. Formerly an ideal society based on principles was accepted – for instance – a corporative society. This has been been abandoned by the opinion that an ideal theoretical society simply does not exist. This change in view in the nature of social criticism contains a denial of its own past, which after all may repeat itself in the future and which excludes certainty about oneself.

This denial need not occur, when in the first place the critical ideology is accepted as the only real form of social criticism and subsequently it can be assumed that this has been dressed in an analytical appearance for a specific historical phase. An accounting of criticism in the manner here suggested – comprehensible within the limits of place and time – is based on freedom and equality. The freedom is a condition for the establishment of social criticism, with relation to which the designer can be made responsible; an equality cannot be ignored in order to achieve progress of this accounting in a correct manner in a social connection. In the light of this, the question is raised whether critical ideology allows room for such freedom and equality as are necessary as a foundation for a correct social criticism. When answering this it can simultaneously be shown whether a methodological reorientation based on the critical ideology is desirable or not. On the one hand this ideology – as a contemporary matter – always contains a link between the present and the past; on the other hand the method of the moment is a historical matter – as was already apparent from the evolution of the classical school up to Marshall. In fact this concerns the question whether the ideology concerned provides a methodological foundation following the indicated line of development. From now on attention is directed towards critical ideology as a two-fold matter. In the first instance, it must be investigated whether it provides, in the correct manner, room for freedom and equality, in the sense that it enables social criticism to be accounted for. Additionally, we wonder whether the revision of the economic-scientific method caused by the critical ideology, follows the methodological developments from Comte to Popper (the old positivism to the critical rationalism); or from Smith to Marshall respectively.

According to the old positivism – when science is directed towards the recording of entirely certain knowledge – only one analytical ideology can be accepted, namely the one, which guarantees entirely certain knowledge. Whoever formulates this ideology, pretends to be able to speak with absolute truth, which includes absolute freedom for him, to which others are subjected. In this situation there is a clear lack of freedom and equality, which are necessary for accountable social criticism. Additionally, the possibilities for any of us to pursue a free science are minimal.

The changeover from the old positivism to critical rationalism means an improvement to such an extent that thereby an analytical ideological equality was created. After all, with that changeover everybody acquired the freedom to determine his social criticism without any further accounting in a social connection. Even though this changeover must be admired, the desired freedom and equality were not reached. After all, it only provided the possibility of remaining faithful to the contents of a social critical point of view, by not divorcing itself from the once accepted analytical ideology. However, this requires in the present social-economic order the retention of a non-rationally justified social concept, which gradually and visibly dates. Obviously, this situation forms a possible source of serious generation conflicts. The deepest cause of the problems – that now becomes apparent – is in the nature of the critical ideology. After all, this means that the time during which a social criticism is valid for its contents does not belong to the region covered by the free human power of decision. This presents the heart of the problem and the beginning of a possible solution.

It means also that the period during which a certain form of social criticism has relevance to its contents can be indicated by us. With an extension of the 'force to initiative' in that manner a freedom and equality are reached in principle, which allows a change in social criticism to take place when a changed historical situation gives rise to this, without this having to cause a denial of the past. However, in fact this presents an acceptance of a critical ideology; as such this allows for the desired freedom and equality. And because it provides the type of essential correction to the analytical ideology which is necessary after the evolution from Smith to Marshall, it follows historically the methodological development, as this took place so far within the economy. In the actual execution of a methodological re-orientation as indicated here, mainly three points require attention:

- the neo-marxian critical theory, which developed within the Frankfurter School must be rejected as a fundamental point for the methodological renewal. The scientific theory concerned is characterized by a historic predisposition and future perspective which is too limited, as it has been accepted a priori that social criticism within the limits of science must always have a marxian-flavoured emancipation tendency. In this, the time during which a specific society criticism is valid for its contents has not been made the object of free decision in the correct manner;
- the convincing architectonic criticism acquires a good deal of attention. It includes a reference to undesirable power concentrations, the costs of economic growth, a suspect directiveness of the production pattern and the non-harmonic prosperity development in the world. With a revision of the method as described above, this criticism acquires a stable place in economic science;
- the four methodological fundamental points – the system of data choice and description, the application of mathematical methods, the distribution of work between micro and macro economy and the historical dependence – must be subjected to great changes. An introductory description of these changes in general and relating to the theory of international trade in particular is provided in para 3 of chapter VI.

The possible revision of the economic-scientific method as discussed here, forms an application of the critical method.

BIBLIOGRAPHY

Baily, Martin J., *National Income and the Price Level.* New York 1972.

Batra, R. N., *Studies in the Theory of International Trade.* London 1973.

Benham, F., The terms of trade. *Economica.* Band 7, 1940.

Binswanger, H. C., *Markt und internationale Währungsordnung.* (Market and the international monetary system). Zürich 1969.

Cairnes, J. E., *Some Leading Principles of Political Economy Newly Expounded.* London 1884.

Caves, Richard E., *Trade and Economic Structure.* London 1960.

Clark, J. B., *The Distribution of Wealth.* London 1920.

Edgeworth, F. J., *Papers Relating to Political Economy.* Volume II. New York 1925.

Enke, Stephen and Virgil Salera, *International economics.* London z.j.

Eucken, Walter, *Die Grundlagen der Nationalökonomie.* (Principles of national economy). Berlin 1950.

Fowle, Lawrence W., *International Trade and Commercial Policy.* New York/London 1948.

Freeman, A. Myrick, *International Trade: an Introduction to Method and Theory.* New York 1971.

Gevel, A. W. J. van de, *Internationale handel en economische groei.* (International trade and economic growth). Tilburg 1970.

Graham, Frank D., *The Theory of International Values.* Princeton 1948.

Gray, Alexander, *The Development of Economic Doctrine.* London 1931.

Haberler, Gottfried von, *The Theory of International Trade.* London 1950.

Hague, Douglas C. and Stonier, Alfred W., *A Textbook of Economic Theory.* London 1956.

Harris, Seymour E., *International and Interregional Economics.* New York 1957.

Harrod, R., *International Economics.* London/Cambridge 1952.

Heller, H. Robert, *International Trade; Theory and Empirical Evidence.* New Jersey 1968.

Ingram - John Kells, *Geschichte der Volkswirtschaftslehre.* (History of economic theory). Tübingen 1890.

Janssen S. J., L. H., *Free Trade, Protection and Customs Union.* Leiden 1961.

Johnson, Harry G., *Money, Trade and Economic Growth.* London 1964.

Jong, A. M. de, *Internationale handel en handelspolitiek.* (International trade and commercial policy). 's-Gravenhage 1937.

Kemp, M. C., *The Pure Theory of International Trade.* Homewood, Ill. 1964.

Ketting, A., *Inleiding tot de handelstheorie* (Introduction to commercial theory). Rotterdam 1973.

Klant, J. J., *Spelregels voor economen.* (Rules for economists). Leiden 1973.

Kohimey, Gunther und Autoren-Kollektiv, *Nationale Produktivität; dynamische Produktionen; internationale Wirtschaft.* (National productivity, dynamic productions, international economy). Berlin 1966.

Korteweg, S. en Keesing, F. A. G., *Het moderne geldwezen.* (The modern monetary system). Amsterdam 1971.

Lipsey, Richard G. and Steiner, Peter O., *Economics*. London 1972.
Marshall, Alfred, *Money, Credit and Commerce*. London 1924.
Marshall, Alfred, *The Pure Theory of Foreign Trade. The Pure Theory of Domestic Values*. London 1926.
Meade, James Edward, *A Geometry of International Trade*. London 1952.
Meier, Gerard M., *International Trade and Development*. New York 1964.
Mill, J. S., *Principles of Political Economy*. (Original 1848). London 1886.
Ohlin, Bertil, *Interregional and International Trade*. Cambridge 1933.
Pearce, S. F., *International Trade*. London 1970.
Plattel, M. G., *Sociale wijsbegeerte*, I. (Social philosophy). Utrecht 1961.
Ricardo, David, *The Principles of Political Economy and Taxation*. (Original 1817). London 1965.
Robbins, L., *An Essay on the Nature and Significance of Economic Science*. London 1972.
Roos, F. de, *Theorie van de internationale economische betrekkingen*. (Theory of international economic relations). Haarlem 1971.
Rose, Klaus (Herausgeber), *Theorie der internationalen Wirtschaftsbeziehungen*. (Theory of international economic relations). Köln/Berlin 1965.
Rose, Klaus, *Theorie des Aussenwirtschaft*. (Theory of foreign trade). Berlin/Frankfurt a.M. 1970.
Rijnvos, C. J., *Economische orde en Europese monetaire integratie*. (Economic system and European monetary integration). Leiden 1970.
Rijnvos, C. J., *Waardering van het economische denken*. (Valuation of economic science). Leiden 1972.
Salera, Vergil, see Enke.
Samuelson, P. A., see Stolper.
Samuelson, P. A., *International Factor-Price Equalisation Once Again*. In: Readings in International Economics. London 1969. (Original publication in: *Economic Journal*, June 1949).
Schneider, Erich, *Einführung in die Wirtschaftstheorie*, II. Teil. (Introduction into the economic theory, part II). Tübingen 1961.
Schouten, D. B. J., *Exacte economie*. (Exact economics). Leiden 1957.
Shone, R., *The Pure Theory of International Trade*. Tripteer 1972.
Södersten, Bo, *A Study of Economic Growth and International Trade*. Stockholm 1964.
Södersten, Bo, *International economics*. London 1973.
Stolper, W. S. and Samuelson, P. A., *Protection and Real Wages*. Originally: Review of Economic Studies, vol. 9, 1941, page 58-73.
Stonier, Alfred W. and Hague, Douglas C., *A Textbook of Economic Theory*. London 1956.
Viner, Jacob, *Studies in the Theory of International Trade*. London/New York 1937.
Wells, Sidney J., *International Economics*. London 1970.
Wemelsfelder, J., *Internationale economische betrekkingen*. (International economic relations). In: *Repertorium van de sociale wetenschappen*. Amsterdam 1959.
Whale, Barret, *International Trade*. London 1934.
Zwiedineck-Südenhorst, O. von, *Mensch und Wirtschaft*. (Man and economy). Berlin 1955.

INDEX